America's Best
Bed & Breakfast Recipes

*French Toast Stuffed
with Bananas
and Walnuts*

Page 52

*Jeanne's Pumpkin
Squares*

Page 104

Our Favorite Recipes
Hand Picked For You

Printed in the United States of America
by G&R Publishing Co.

Distributed By:

507 Industrial Street
Waverly, IA 50677

ISBN 1-56383-177-5
Item # 3801

Table of Contents

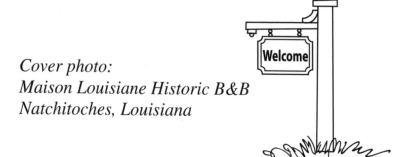

Cover photo:
Maison Louisiane Historic B&B
Natchitoches, Louisiana

Beverages,
Sauces & Snacks

Spice Tea

1 1/3 C. Tang
1/2 C. sugar
1/3 C. instant tea

1 tsp. cinnamon
1/2 tsp. ground cloves

In a large bowl, combine Tang, sugar, instant tea, cinnamon and ground cloves. Store in an airtight container. Add 2 teaspoons Spice Tea mixture to 1 cup of hot water. Stir and enjoy.

Sheep Hill B&B and Antique Shop
East Earl, Pennsylvania

Blushing Orange Cooler

1 (6 oz.) can frozen orange juice concentrate
1 C. cranberry juice cocktail

1/4 C. sugar
1 C. crushed ice
1 C. club soda

In a blender, combine frozen orange juice concentrate, cranberry juice cocktail and sugar. Mix until well blended. Place crushed ice in a tall glass. Pour orange juice puree over ice. Pour club soda over liquid in glass. Stir slightly and serve.

Roses & the River Inc. B&B
Brazoria, Texas

3

Cranberry-Orange Frappe

2 C. cranberry juice
1 C. orange juice
1/4 C. whipped cream
Sugar to taste

1 T. lemon juice
2 bananas
3/4 C. crushed ice
Mint leaves

In a blender, combine cranberry juice, orange juice, whipped cream, sugar, lemon juice, bananas and crushed ice. Process on high for 1 minute. Serve in stemmed goblets and garnish with mint leaves.

Aleksander House B&B
Louisville, Kentucky

Strawberry Surprise

2 C. fresh or frozen strawberries, sliced
2 C. crushed ice

1/2 C. white wine or Vernor's ginger ale
Sugar to taste

In a blender, combine strawberries, crushed ice and white wine. Blend until smooth. Add sugar to taste. Serve as a smoothie for breakfast.

Variation
This recipe can be frozen and served as a sherbet for dessert or as a palate refresher between heavy courses. More liquid can be added to this recipe to create a cold soup. Add a dollop of yogurt before serving.

Iron Mountain Inn B&B and Creekside Chalet
Butler, Tennessee

Easy Lemon Curd

Makes 1 3/4 cups

4 egg yolks
1 egg, lightly beaten
1 C. sugar

1/2 C. lemon juice
1/2 C. butter
1 tsp. grated lemon peel

In a medium heavy saucepan, whisk egg yolks and egg until smooth. Add sugar and lemon juice, whisking until well mixed. Cook slowly over low medium heat, stirring constantly, until mixture thickens enough to coat back of wooden spoon, approximately 10 to 12 minutes. Remove from heat. Cut butter into small pieces and stir, one piece at a time, into warm mixture until melted and fully absorbed. Stir in grated lemon peel. Serve warm with waffles, pancakes and crepes. Serve cold as a parfait layer or topping for fresh fruit, tarts and cakes.

River House B&B Inn & Tepee
Rockford – Machesney Park, Illinois

Apple Cider Syrup

1/2 C. sugar
4 tsp. cornstarch
1 tsp. cinnamon
1 C. apple cider or apple
   juice

1 T. lemon juice
2 T. butter or margarine

In a small saucepan, combine sugar, cornstarch and cinnamon. Stir in apple cider and lemon juice. Cook, stirring constantly, over medium heat until mixture is thickened and bubbly. Cook and stir for an additional 2 minutes. Remove saucepan from heat and stir in butter or margarine until melted. Serve over waffles or pancakes.

Sunrise Farm B&B
Salem, South Carolina

Blueberry Sauce

Makes 2 cups

2 C. fresh or frozen
   blueberries
1/2 C. sugar
1/2 C. water
1/2 tsp. salt

1/2 tsp. cinnamon
1 T. cornstarch
1 T. lemon juice
1/2 T. lime juice

In a medium saucepan over medium heat, combine blueberries, sugar, water, salt and cinnamon. Bring to a boil. Reduce heat and let simmer until blueberries are tender, about 15 minutes. In a separate bowl, blend cornstarch with lemon and lime juice. As soon as berries are boiling, add cornstarch mixture to saucepan, stirring constantly. Sauce will thicken and become clear in about 3 minutes. Let cool and store in an airtight container in refrigerator. Serve with pancakes or waffles.

Hillside Farm B&B
Mount Joy, Pennsylvania

8

Chocolate Mousse Crepe Filling

6 oz. semisweet or
  bittersweet chocolate,
  chopped
3 T. unsalted butter
2 T. liquor, liqueur, coffee
  or water
1 tsp. vanilla (only if
  using water)

3 large eggs, separated
3 T. coffee or water
1/4 C. plus 3 T. sugar,
  divided
1/4 tsp. cream of tartar
1/2 C. cold heavy cream
1 qt. fresh strawberries,
  diced

In a large skillet, heat 1" water over low heat until bubbles form along the bottom. Adjust the heat to maintain the water at this temperature. In a large heat-proof bowl, combine chocolate, butter and liquid. Set the bowl in the water bath and stir until chocolate is melted. Remove from water and set aside. In another heat-proof bowl, whisk together egg yolks, coffee or water and 3 tablespoons sugar. Set the bowl in the water bath. Whisking constantly, heat the mixture until thick and puffy. Remove from water bath and whisk thoroughly into melted chocolate. Let mixture cool to room temperature. In a mixing bowl, beat egg whites at medium speed until foamy. Add cream of tartar and beat until soft peaks form. Gradually beat in remaining 1/4 cup sugar. Increase the speed to high and beat until the peaks are stiff. Using a large rubber spatula, stir 1/4 of the egg whites into the chocolate mixture. Gently fold in the remaining egg whites. In a separate mixing bowl, beat heavy cream at medium high speed until soft peaks form. Gently but thoroughly fold the cream into the chocolate mixture. Transfer to a medium bowl. Refrigerate at least 4 hours or overnight. Carefully fold diced strawberries into prepared chocolate mousse. Can use as filling for French Style Crepes (page 40).

Maison Louisiane Historic B&B
Natchitoches, Louisiana

A Granola to Make You Smile

1 C. honey
1 C. light vegetable oil
12 C. old fashioned
   oats
2 C. chopped walnuts
   or pecans

2 C. chopped almonds
1 C. All-Bran cereal
1 C. shredded coconut
6 T. cinnamon
2 C. raisins

Preheat oven to 325°. In a medium saucepan over medium heat, bring honey and oil to near boiling. In a large roasting pan, combine oatmeal, chopped walnuts or pecans, chopped almonds, All-Bran cereal, coconut flakes and cinnamon. Pour hot honey and oil mixture, stirring constantly, over dry ingredients in roasting pan. Bake for 40 minutes, stirring every 10 minutes, until golden brown. Let cool and mix in raisins.

Dupont at The Circle - a B&B Inn
Washington, D.C.

Layered Shrimp Dip

Makes 12 to 16 servings

1 (3 oz.) pkg. cream
 cheese, softened
6 T. salsa, divided
1/2 C. cocktail sauce
1 lb. shrimp, chopped
 to 1/2" pieces
1 (2 1/4 oz.) can sliced
 black olives, drained

1 C. shredded Cheddar
 cheese
1 C. shredded Monterey
 Jack cheese
Sliced green onions
Tortilla chips or crackers

In a medium bowl, combine cream cheese and 3 tablespoons salsa. Spread mixture into an ungreased 9" pie pan. In a separate bowl, combine remaining 3 tablespoons salsa and cocktail sauce. Spread cocktail sauce mixture over cream cheese layer in pan. Place shrimp pieces evenly over layers in pan. Sprinkle sliced olives over shrimp. In a separate bowl, combine shredded Cheddar cheese and shredded Monterey Jack cheese. Sprinkle cheese mixture over olives. Top with sliced green onions. Chill in refrigerator and serve with tortilla chips or crackers.

Big Moose Inn B&B
Eagle Bay, New York

Aunt Edna's Granola

1 C. honey
1 C. oil
5 C. old fashioned oats
1 C. sunflower seeds
1 C. sesame seeds

1 C. powdered milk
1 C. slivered almonds
1 C. wheat germ
1 C. soy flour

Preheat oven to 400°. In a large bowl, combine honey and oil. Add oats, sunflower seeds, sesame seeds, powdered milk, slivered almonds, wheat germ and soy flour. Stir all together. Place in an oven-safe bowl or pan and bake for 40 minutes, stirring after each 8 to 10 minutes of baking time. Store in an airtight container.

Variation
If desired, add 1 cup dried fruit after baking or 1 cup raw cashews before baking.

Amanda Gish House B&B
Elizabethtown, Pennsylvania

Swiss Cheese Fondue

1 clove garlic, crushed
12 oz. dry white wine
14 oz. grated
   Emmenthaler cheese
14 oz. grated Gruyere
   cheese

3 tsp. Kirsch schnapps
2 tsp. potato flour
Fresh ground pepper and
   nutmeg
2 lbs. white bread, cut into
   small cubes

Rub the inside of a heat-proof casserole dish with crushed garlic. Add white wine and warm over low heat on stovetop. Add grated cheeses and bring to a boil over medium heat. Stir with a rubber spatula until cheese is melted. In a small bowl, combine Kirsch schnapps and potato flour, stirring until smooth. Stir mixture into cheeses in casserole dish. Season with pepper and nutmeg to taste. Remove casserole dish from stovetop and place over a fondue burner. Serve with bread cubes for dipping, stirring often.

Waterloo Country Inn
Princess Anne, Maryland

Apple Cranberry Granola

6 C. old fashioned oats
1 1/4 C. apple juice
   concentrate
1/2 C. wheat germ
1/2 C. brown sugar
2 1/2 to 3 T. cinnamon
1 C. sunflower seeds

1 C. shredded coconut
1 1/2 C. sliced almonds
1 T. vanilla
1 C. dried cranberries
1/2 C. raisins
1/2 C. golden raisins

In a large bowl, combine oats, apple juice concentrate, wheat germ, brown sugar, cinnamon, sunflower seeds, shredded coconut, sliced almonds and vanilla. Mix well and spread mixture evenly into 2 lightly greased 9x13" baking dishes. Bake for 20 minutes and stir gently. Return to oven for an additional 15 minutes. Bake until golden brown, being careful not to burn granola on bottom of pan. Remove from oven and let granola cool slightly before adding dried cranberries, raisins and golden raisins. Store in an airtight container.

Inn at Valley Farms B&B and Cottages
Walpole, New Hampshire

Gingered Pineapple Salsa with Toasted Coconut

1 (20 oz.) can pineapple chunks, drained
1 (20 oz.) can crushed pineapple, drained
1 C. shredded coconut, toasted*
1 C. thinly sliced scallions, green part only
1/4 C. seeded and chopped jalapeno peppers, optional
1 1/2 tsp. fresh minced gingerroot
1/2 C. water
1/2 C. sugar
1 T. salt
Zest and juice of 2 lemons
1/2 C. fresh chopped cilantro

In a large bowl, combine drained pineapple chunks, drained crushed pineapple, toasted coconut, sliced scallions, chopped jalapeno peppers, minced gingerroot, water, sugar, salt, zest and juice of lemons and fresh chopped cilantro. Mix well and refrigerate until ready to serve. Serve with tortilla chips

* To toast, place shredded coconut in a single layer on a baking sheet. Bake at 350° for approximately 10 minutes or until coconut is golden brown.

The White Rose B&B Inn
Wisconsin Dells, Wisconsin

15

Gourmet Granola

6 C. old fashioned oats	1/2 C. light oil
1/2 C. chopped pecans	1/2 C. brown sugar
1 C. chopped walnuts	1/2 C. honey
1/2 C. sesame seeds	1/2 C. maple syrup
3/4 C. sunflower seeds	1/4 C. molasses
1 C. shredded coconut	1 T. vanilla
1/2 C. raisins	1 1/2 tsp. cinnamon
1/2 C. dried cranberries	1/2 tsp. salt

Preheat oven to 350°. In a large roasting pan, combine oats, pecans, walnuts, sesame seeds and sunflower seeds. Heat in oven until lightly toasted, about 8 to 10 minutes. Remove from oven and let cool. In a large bowl, combine toasted mixture, shredded coconut, raisins and cranberries. Set aside. In a large saucepan over low heat, combine oil, brown sugar, honey, syrup, molasses, vanilla, cinnamon and salt. Heat, stirring frequently, until mixture is combined, being careful not to boil. Pour liquid mixture over ingredients in bowl. Mix until evenly coated and spread mixture onto a greased baking sheet. Bake for 30 minutes, stirring after every 5 minutes. Remove from oven, let cool and store in an airtight container.

Chambered Nautilus B&B Inn
Seattle, Washington

16

Breads & Sides

Bacon Cheese Muffins

1 3/4 C. flour
1 tsp. baking powder
1/2 tsp. salt
1 T. sugar
1/2 tsp. baking soda
1/8 tsp. garlic powder
1 C. shredded Cheddar
   cheese

8 slices bacon, cooked
   and crumbled
2 T. bacon drippings
1 C. sour cream
1 egg, beaten
2 T. milk
2 tsp. sesame seeds

Preheat oven to 400°. Into a large bowl, sift flour, baking powder, salt, sugar, baking soda and garlic powder. Stir in shredded Cheddar cheese and crumbled bacon. In a small bowl, beat together bacon drippings, sour cream, beaten egg and milk. Stir sour cream mixture into dry ingredients. Mix until batter is well blended. Fill the cups of a greased muffin tin 2/3 full with batter. Sprinkle sesame seeds over batter in muffin cups. Bake for 20 to 25 minutes, until golden brown.

Magnolia Grove B&B
Hernando, Mississippi

Sweet Potato Muffins

1/2 C. butter, softened
1 1/4 C. sugar
2 eggs
1 1/4 C. mashed sweet
  potatoes
2 tsp. baking powder
1/4 tsp. salt

1 tsp. cinnamon
1/4 tsp. nutmeg
1 C. milk
1/4 C. pecans
1/2 C. golden raisins
1 1/2 C. flour

Preheat oven to 400°. In a large bowl, cream butter and sugar. Add eggs, mashed sweet potatoes, baking powder, salt, cinnamon, nutmeg, milk, pecans, golden raisins and flour. Mix just until batter is moistened. Transfer batter to greased muffin tins and bake for 15 to 20 minutes.

Elson Inn B&B
Magnolia, Ohio

Blue Corn Muffins with Chile and Cheese

1/2 C. butter, softened
1/2 C. sugar
5 large eggs
1/2 C. buttermilk or
   milk
1 C. flour
1 C. blue cornmeal
2 tsp. baking powder

1 tsp. salt
1 C. corn kernels, canned
   or frozen
1 C. shredded Monterey
   Jack cheese
1 C. shredded Cheddar
   cheese
3/4 C. diced roasted chilies

Preheat oven to 375°. Grease muffin tins or fill with paper liners. In a medium mixing bowl, cream butter and sugar until smooth. In a large bowl, whisk together eggs and buttermilk. In a separate bowl, combine flour, blue cornmeal, baking powder and salt. Fold dry ingredients into butter and sugar mixture. Fold batter into eggs and buttermilk mixture. Stir in corn kernels, shredded Monterey Jack cheese, shredded Cheddar cheese and diced roasted chilies. Mix until well blended. Spoon batter into prepared muffin tins. Bake for 25 minutes, until just firm. Serve muffins warm with butter.

Good Life Inn B&B
High Rolls, New Mexico

Banana Bran Muffins

1 egg
3/4 C. brown sugar
1 1/3 C. mashed ripe
   bananas
1/2 C. walnuts
1/3 C. vegetable oil
1 tsp. vanilla
3/4 C. flour

3/4 C. whole wheat flour
1/2 C. oat bran or
   unprocessed wheat bran
2 tsp. baking powder
1/2 tsp. baking soda
1 tsp. cinnamon
1/4 tsp. salt

Preheat oven to 350°. Grease the cups of 1 regular or 2 mini muffin tins and set aside. In medium mixing bowl, beat egg and brown sugar until smooth. Add mashed bananas, walnuts, vegetable oil and vanilla. Mix well and let stand 1 minute. In a large bowl, combine flour, whole wheat flour, oat bran, baking powder, baking soda, cinnamon and salt. Using a spatula, fold banana mixture into dry ingredients, just until moistened. Scoop batter into greased muffin cups. Bake for 15 to 25 minutes, until brown and springy to the touch. Turn muffins out onto a rack to cool.

Hillside Farm B&B
Mount Joy, Pennsylvania

21

Whole Wheat Buttermilk Rolls

1 pkg. dry yeast
1 C. warmed buttermilk
3 T. shortening
1 tsp. brown sugar

1/4 tsp. baking soda
2 1/4 C. wheat flour
1 tsp. baking powder
1 1/4 T. salt

Preheat oven to 425°. In a medium bowl, dissolve yeast in warmed buttermilk. Blend in shortening, brown sugar and baking soda. In a separate bowl, combine wheat flour, baking powder and salt. Add flour mixture to buttermilk mixture and stir for 1 minute. Cover and let rise until mixture has doubled in volume. Punch down dough and let rise again until doubled. Knead dough for 10 minutes. Roll dough into 1" balls and place 3 balls in each cup of greased muffin tins. Cover tins with a damp cloth and let rise to desired height. Bake for 15 to 20 minutes, until golden brown.

Big Moose Inn B&B
Eagle Bay, New York

Cream Biscuits

Makes 10 biscuits

2 C. flour	**1/2 tsp. salt**
1 T. baking powder	**1 1/4 C. heavy cream**
3 T. sugar	**Milk or butter for brushing**

Preheat oven to 425°. Into a medium bowl, sift flour, baking powder, sugar and salt. Add heavy cream and stir until mixture forms a dough. Gather dough into a ball and gently knead dough 6 times on a flat floured surface. Roll or pat dough to 1/2" thickness. Cut out rounds with a 2 1/2" round cutter dipped in flour. If desired, cut dough into 10 squares. Transfer biscuits to an ungreased baking sheet. Roll out dough scraps and cut into rounds until there are 10 biscuits. Brush tops of biscuits with milk or butter and bake for 15 minutes, until pale golden. Transfer biscuits to a wire rack and let cool for 5 minutes.

Rock Cottage Gardens... a Bed & Breakfast Inn
Eureka Springs, Arkansas

Homespun Sweet and Sunny Cornbread

3/4 C. sugar	1 1/2 C. cornmeal
1/2 C. oil	3 C. milk, divided
2 eggs	Pinch of dried thyme
1 1/2 C. plus 3 1/2 T. flour, divided	Pinch of marjoram
3 tsp. baking powder	1/4 C. frozen corn
1/2 tsp. plus 1/8 tsp. salt, divided	4 T. butter, softened
	4 boiled eggs, chopped
	Paprika for garnish

Preheat oven to 400°. In a large bowl, combine sugar, oil and eggs. Mix well and add 1 1/2 cups flour, baking powder, 1/8 teaspoon salt, cornmeal and 1 cup milk. Mix well and add thyme and marjoram. Mix in frozen corn. Transfer batter to a greased 9" square pan. Bake for 30 minutes. To make white sauce, in a medium saucepan over medium heat, combine butter and remaining 3 1/2 tablespoons flour, stirring until melted. Remove from heat and let cool 1 minute. Add remaining 2 cups milk, remaining 1/2 teaspoon salt and most of the chopped boiled eggs. When cornbread is done, pour white sauce with eggs over each serving on plate. Top each serving with some of the remaining chopped eggs and a pinch of paprika.

Homespun Farm B&B
Griswold, Connecticut

Strawberry Bread

Makes 2 loaves

3 C. flour	1 1/4 C. vegetable oil
2 C. sugar	2 (10 oz.) pkgs. frozen
1 tsp. baking soda	strawberries, thawed
1 tsp. salt	and chopped
1 tsp. cinnamon	1 C. chopped pecans,
4 eggs, beaten	optional

In a large bowl, combine flour, sugar, baking soda, salt and cinnamon, forming a well in the center of the mixture. In a separate bowl, combine beaten eggs, vegetable oil, strawberries and chopped pecans. Pour into well in dry ingredients and stir until evenly blended. Spoon mixture into 2 greased and floured 5x9" loaf pans. Bake for 1 hour. Let loaves cool in pans for 10 minutes. Remove to wire racks and let cool completely. Freezes well.

Variation
Substitute 2 cups fresh or frozen strawberries for frozen packages of strawberries.

Frosting

1 1/3 C. box powdered	1 tsp. vanilla
sugar,	9 to 10 T. butter, softened
4 oz. cream cheese,	Chopped nuts, optional
softened	

In a medium bowl, combine powdered sugar, cream cheese, vanilla, butter and chopped nuts. Spread frosting over cooled bread.

Harmony Hill B&B
Arrington, Virginia

Apricot Bread

Makes 2 loaves

2 jars apricot baby food
1 C. vegetable oil
1 C. buttermilk
3 eggs
2 1/2 C. flour

2 C. sugar
2 tsp. baking soda
1 tsp. cinnamon
1/2 tsp. salt

Preheat oven to 350°. In a large bowl, combine apricot baby food, vegetable oil, buttermilk and eggs. Add flour, sugar, baking soda, cinnamon and salt. Mix until well blended. Pour mixture into 2 greased loaf pans. Bake for 60 minutes or until a toothpick inserted in center of bread comes out clean.

The Steamboat House B&B
Galena, Illinois

Momma's Cornbread

1 1/4 C. flour
3/4 C. cornmeal
4 tsp. baking powder
1/2 tsp. salt

1/4 C. sugar
1 egg
1 C. milk
1 T. butter, melted

Preheat oven to 425°. In a large bowl, combine flour, cornmeal, baking powder, salt, sugar, egg, milk and melted butter. Mix well. Transfer to a greased 8x8" pan. Bake for 15 to 20 minutes or until a toothpick inserted in center comes out clean.

Parsonage on the Green B&B
Lee, Massachusetts

Pull-Apart Bread

1 pkg. frozen yeast dinner rolls	1 C. brown sugar
	2 T. cinnamon
1 (3 1/2 oz.) pkg. butterscotch pudding mix	1/2 C. butter, melted
	1/2 C. pecans, optional

Grease a loaf or bundt pan and layer frozen dinner rolls over bottom of pan. Spread butterscotch pudding mix evenly over rolls in pan. Sprinkle brown sugar and cinnamon evenly over pudding mix. Pour melted butter over sugar and cinnamon. If desired, sprinkle pecans evenly over butter. Cover pan and let sit overnight in oven. In the morning, bake bread at 350° for about 30 minutes. Remove pan from oven and turn over onto serving plate. To serve, cut bread into pieces or pull pieces from   bread.

Homespun Farm B&B
Griswold, Connecticut

Indian Fry Bread

4 C. flour　　　　　　**6 tsp. baking powder**
2 tsp. salt　　　　　　**1 to 2 T. shortening**

In a medium bowl, combine flour, salt, baking powder and shortening. Add enough water to make a medium stiff dough. Roll dough into a ball about 3" in diameter. Pull into a 6" circle with fingers. Do not use rolling pin. In a skillet, heat 1" cooking oil. When oil is hot, drop dough into skillet. Brown bread on both sides.

Harmony Hill B&B
Arrington, Virginia

29

Smothered Cottage Fries

Makes 6 to 8 servings

6 medium potatoes
2 T. oil
4 T. butter, softened

2 T. Cajun seasoning
1 T. garlic powder

Chop potatoes into 3/4" long pieces that are about 1/4" thick. In a large saucepan, deep fry potatoes in oil, until golden brown. Remove potatoes from oil and place in a large bowl. Add butter, Cajun seasoning and garlic powder. Toss until well mixed. If butter does not melt right away, place bowl in 250° oven for 10 minutes and toss again. Serve and enjoy.

Maison Louisiane Historic B&B
Natchitoches, Louisiana

Mom Huff's Famous Sweet Pickle Chips

8 lbs. cucumber pickles,
  sliced 1/4" thick
4 C. dusting lime
4 lbs. brown sugar
6 C. cider vinegar

2 T. salt
1 T. celery seed
1 T. whole cloves
1 cinnamon stick

In a large bowl, place sliced cucumbers. Pour lime over pickles and add water to cover. Let stand overnight. Pour off water and rinse pickles in cold water until all the lime is washed off. Cover pickles with clean water and let stand for 1 hour. Repeat this procedure three times to assure all the lime is washed off. In a large pot, bring brown sugar, vinegar, salt, celery seed, cloves and cinnamon stick to a boil. Stir in cucumber slices. Remove from heat and let stand overnight. Drain syrup off pickles into a separate pot. Bring pot with syrup to a boil. Place pickles in boiling syrup and let simmer for 1 hour. If desired, pickle chips can be canned while hot. Serve cold.

Iron Mountain Inn B&B and Creekside Chalet
Butler, Tennessee

31

Broccoli Casserole

1 1/2 lbs. fresh broccoli, washed and chopped (or 2 pkgs. frozen), divided
2 eggs, beaten
1 small onion, finely chopped

1 can cream of mushroom soup
1/4 C. mayonnaise
1 C. shredded Cheddar cheese, divided
1 1/2 C. herbed stuffing mix
1/4 C. butter, melted

Preheat oven to 350°. Cook broccoli in boiling water. In a medium bowl, combine beaten eggs, chopped onions, mushroom soup and mayonnaise. In a 2-quart casserole dish, place a layer of half of the broccoli followed by a layer of half of the shredded Cheddar cheese. Pour 1/3 of the mushroom soup mixture over the cheese. Repeat layers with remaining broccoli and remaining shredded Cheddar cheese. Cover with remaining 2/3 of the mushroom soup mixture. Sprinkle stuffing mix over all. Top with melted butter. Bake for 30 minutes.

Cocalico Creek B&B
Denver, Pennsylvania

Corn Pudding

1 box Jiffy corn muffin
   mix
2 eggs
1 C. sour cream
1 (16 oz.) can kernel
   corn, drained

1 (16 oz.) can creamed
   corn
Shredded Swiss cheese

Preheat oven to 350°. In a medium bowl, combine corn muffin mix, eggs, sour cream, drained corn and creamed corn. Place mixture in an ungreased 8" or 9" square baking dish. Bake for 30 to 35 minutes. Remove from oven and sprinkle with desired amount of shredded Swiss cheese. Return to oven and bake an additional 10 minutes.

Sheep Hill B&B and Antique Shop
East Earl, Pennsylvania

33

Apple Pecan Tossed Salad

1 pkg. Good Seasons
   gourmet Caesar salad
   dressing
Apple cider vinegar
Extra virgin olive oil
1 head lettuce
1 medium sweet red
   pepper, seeded and diced

1 large Granny Smith
   apple, cored and diced
2/3 C. chopped pecans,
   toasted*
2/3 C. crumbled blue
   cheese

Prepare Good Seasons gourmet Caesar salad dressing according to package directions, using apple cider vinegar and olive oil. Wash head of lettuce, tear into small pieces and place in a large salad bowl. Toss lettuce with diced sweet red peppers, diced apples, toasted pecans and crumbled blue cheese. Just before serving, add small amounts of dressing to salad and toss until very lightly coated.

* To toast, place pecans in a single layer on a baking sheet. Bake at 350° for approximately 10 minutes or until pecans are golden brown.

Tunnel Mountain B&B
Elkins, West Virginia

34

Asparagus Bundles
with Hollandaise

Makes 6 servings

6 thin slices Swiss cheese	**1/2 C. plus 1 T. butter,**
6 slices cooked ham	**melted, divided**
1 (10 oz.) can asparagus	**3 egg yolks**
spears, drained	**2 T. lemon juice**
1/2 (17 1/2 oz.) pkg. frozen	
puff pastry, thawed	

Preheat oven to 425°. Place 1 slice Swiss cheese over each slice of cooked ham. Top cheese slices with drained asparagus spears. Roll each bundle up, trimming asparagus if necessary. Cut puff pastry into 6 equal triangles. Brush pastry lightly with 1 tablespoon melted butter. Wrap each pastry around cheese, ham and asparagus bundles, sealing at the seam. Place bundles, seam side down, in a shallow lightly greased baking dish. Make sure bundles do not touch each other or sides of pan. Brush tops of pastry with some of the remaining butter. Bake for 18 to 20 minutes, until golden brown. To make Hollandaise sauce, in a blender, combine egg yolks and lemon juice. Puree for 30 seconds. Slowly pour in remaining 1/2 cup hot melted butter while blending, until sauce thickens slightly. Place asparagus bundles on serving plate and drizzle with Hollandaise sauce or serve sauce on the side.

Empress of Little Rock B&B
Little Rock, Arkansas

Squash Soufflé

1/2 C. chopped onion
1/2 C. plus 1 T. butter, divided
1 C. cracker crumbs, divided
1 C. chopped pecans

2 C. cooked baby squash
1/4 C. sugar
1/2 C. mayonnaise
1 C. shredded Cheddar cheese
1 egg, beaten

Preheat oven to 325°. In a medium saucepan over medium heat, sauté chopped onions in 1 tablespoon butter. In a microwave-safe bowl, melt remaining 1/2 cup butter in microwave. Stir in 1/2 cup cracker crumbs and chopped pecans and set aside. In a medium bowl, whip cooked baby squash with an electric mixer. Add sugar, mayonnaise, shredded Cheddar cheese, remaining 1/2 cup cracker crumbs and beaten egg. Mix until blended and pour into a greased casserole dish. Sprinkle topping evenly over squash soufflé. Bake for 45 minutes.

Magnolia Grove B&B
Hernando, Mississippi

Baked Oatmeal

3 C. quick oats
1/2 C. brown sugar
2 eggs
2 C. milk
1/4 tsp. salt
1/2 C. oil
1 tsp. vanilla

1 tsp. cinnamon
1/4 tsp. nutmeg
1 tsp. baking powder
1/2 C. raisins
1/2 C. nuts
1/2 C. diced apples

Preheat oven to 350°. In a large bowl, combine quick oats, brown sugar, eggs, milk, salt, oil, vanilla, cinnamon, nutmeg and baking powder. Mix well. Add raisins, nuts and diced apples and stir until well combined. Pour mixture into a greased 1-quart baking dish. Bake for 45 minutes.

Hillside Farm B&B
Mount Joy, Pennsylvania

Pears in White Zinfandel

8 pears
2 C. White Zinfandel
  wine
2 T. lemon juice
1 C. sugar

2 tsp. cinnamon
Zest of 1 lemon
1 tsp. vanilla
Mint leaves
Crème fraiche

Peel and core pears and set aside. In a deep saucepan, combine White Zinfandel, lemon juice, sugar, cinnamon, lemon zest and vanilla. Bring to a boil. Carefully place each pear, stem up, in saucepan. With a ladle, scoop spoonfuls of liquid mixture over pears. Simmer about 10 to 20 minutes, until pears are tender. Remove pears and place in individual serving dishes. Strain and reserve liquid. Return liquid to heat. Bring to a boil until liquid has reduced by half. Remove from heat and pour wine sauce over pears. Let cool. Garnish with mint leaves. Serve with crème fraiche on the side.

Aleksander House B&B
Louisville, Kentucky

Main Dishes
& Soups

French Style Crepes

Makes 6 to 8 crepes

1/2 C. flour	2 eggs
1/2 C. milk	5 T. unsalted butter,
1/4 C. lukewarm water	melted, divided
1 T. sugar	1 C. maple syrup
Pinch of salt	

In a blender, combine flour, milk, water, sugar, salt, eggs and 2 tablespoons melted butter. Blend until smooth. Let stand for 30 minutes or refrigerate overnight. Grease a 9" crepe pan and hold over medium heat. Pour enough batter to cover the bottom of pan with a thin layer of crepe mixture. Lift pan away from heat and rotate until the batter evenly covers bottom of pan. Cook until top of crepe is set and underside is golden brown. Flip with a spatula or fingers and cook until other side is golden brown. Place crepe on wax paper and repeat until batter is gone. If desired, fill crepes with Chocolate Mousse Crepe Filling (page 9). In a medium saucepan, combine maple syrup and remaining 3 tablespoons melted butter, until warmed. Pour over filled crepes.

Maison Louisiane Historic B&B
Natchitoches, Louisiana

Citrus Waffles

Makes 14 to 16 waffles

2 C. flour	3 eggs, separated
1/4 C. sugar	1 C. buttermilk
2 tsp. baking powder	2/3 C. sour cream
1 tsp. baking soda	1/2 C. butter, melted
1 tsp. salt	Powdered sugar
1 large grapefruit	Fresh or frozen blueberries
1/2 C. orange juice	Sliced almonds to garnish

Preheat waffle iron. In a large mixing bowl, combine flour, sugar, baking powder, baking soda and salt. Cut the grapefruit in half and loosen sections with fruit knife. Squeeze grapefruit juice into measuring cup and fill to 1 cup mark with orange juice. In a separate bowl, whisk together egg yolks, buttermilk, sour cream, melted butter and juice mixture. Pour mixture into dry ingredients, mixing to form a moist batter. In a small mixing bowl, beat egg whites to stiff peaks and gently fold into batter. Pour some of the batter into preheated waffle iron and bake until golden brown. Repeat until batter is gone. Dust with powdered sugar. Sprinkle with blueberries and sliced almonds. If desired, serve immediately with Easy Lemon Curd (page 6) or syrup.

River House B&B Inn & Tepee
Rockford – Machesney Park, Illinois

Fluffy Cinnamon Waffles
with Pecan Syrup

2 C. biscuit mix
1/2 C. oil
1 egg
1/2 tsp. cinnamon
1 1/3 C. club soda
1 C. maple syrup
1 C. dark corn syrup

2 T. bourbon
1 T. butter
1 C. ground pecans,
   toasted*
1 1/2 C. coarsely chopped
   pecans, toasted*

Preheat waffle iron. In a medium bowl, combine biscuit mix, oil, egg, cinnamon and club soda. In hot waffle iron, cook batter and keep waffles warm until syrup is ready. To make syrup, in a medium pan, combine maple syrup, dark corn syrup, bourbon and butter. Bring to a boil over medium high heat. Stir in ground toasted pecans and coarsely chopped pecans and let cool slightly. Pour over hot waffles. Syrup can be stored in refrigerator in an airtight container for up to 1 week.

* To toast, place pecans in a single layer on a baking sheet. Bake at 350° for approximately 10 minutes (less for ground pecans) or until pecans are golden brown.

Tunnel Mountain B&B
Elkins, West Virginia

Gingerbread Waffles

Makes 10 waffles

3 eggs, separated	**1/2 tsp. salt, optional**
1 C. skim milk	**1 tsp. cinnamon**
1/2 C. dark molasses	**1 tsp. ground ginger**
1/2 C. brown sugar	**1/4 tsp. ground cloves**
1 3/4 C. flour	**1/2 C. butter, melted**
4 tsp. baking powder	

Preheat and lightly grease a waffle iron. In a medium bowl, beat egg yolks with a whisk. Stir in milk, molasses and brown sugar until blended. Into a separate bowl, sift flour, baking powder, salt, cinnamon, ground ginger and ground cloves. Add dry ingredients and melted butter to molasses mixture. In a separate bowl, beat egg whites until stiff peaks form. Fold egg whites into batter. Pour 1/10 of the batter onto a hot waffle iron to cook. Repeat with remaining batter.

Deacon Timothy Pratt B&B
Old Saybrook, Connecticut

Wild Rice Quiche

Makes 6 servings

1 (10") unbaked pie shell	2 C. shredded Swiss cheese
1/3 C. chopped onion	1 C. cooked wild rice
1/4 C. chopped red pepper	4 eggs
2 T. butter	1 C. half n' half
1/2 lb. diced smoked turkey	1/2 tsp. salt
	1 T. Worcestershire sauce

Preheat oven to 425°. Place unbaked pie shell in a glass quiche pan. In a medium saucepan over medium heat, sauté onions and red peppers in butter, until onions are transparent. In pie shell, layer turkey, onion mixture, shredded Swiss cheese and rice. In a blender, combine eggs, half n' half, salt and Worcestershire sauce at high speed for 30 seconds. Immediately pour mixture over ingredients in pie shell. Bake for 15 minutes. Reduce heat to 325° and continue baking for an additional 30 minutes. Remove from oven and let sit for 15 minutes before cutting into wedges. Serve warm.

River House B&B Inn & Tepee
Rockford-Machesney Park, Illinois

Atwood House Portabella Mushroom Quiche

Makes 1 serving

1 egg
1/4 C. heavy cream
1/4 C. shredded Swiss
  cheese
1 sausage patty, cooked
  and crumbled

1/4 tsp. Worcestershire
  sauce
Salt and pepper to taste
1 portabella mushroom
  (approximately 4 1/2" to
  5" in diameter)

Preheat oven to 350°. In a medium bowl, combine egg, heavy cream, shredded Swiss cheese, crumbled sausage, Worcestershire sauce, salt and pepper. Remove mushroom stem and dark brown veins from mushroom cap and discard. Place cap, top side down, in a 6" soufflé dish. Pour quiche mixture into mushroom cap. Bake for 30 minutes, until quiche is set.

Atwood House B&B
Lincoln, Nebraska

45

Bear Paw "Killer" Quiche

Makes 6 to 8 servings

1 C. frozen chopped
  spinach, thawed
2 T. butter
1/2 small onion,
  chopped
14 mushrooms, sliced
1 (8" or 9") pie crust
8 oz. cream cheese,
  cut into small pieces

1/4 lb. shredded Swiss
  cheese
1/4 lb. shredded Monterey
  Jack cheese
8 large eggs
1 C. half n' half
1 tsp. nutmeg

Preheat oven to 425°. Squeeze thawed spinach between paper towels to remove water. In a medium pan, melt butter over medium high heat and sauté onions until transparent. Add mushrooms and sauté until browned. Cover the bottom of the pie crust with cream cheese pieces. Add sautéed onions, mushrooms and drained spinach. Top with shredded Swiss and Monterey Jack cheeses. In a medium bowl, combine eggs, half n' half and nutmeg. Pour egg mixture over ingredients in pie pan. Bake quiche for 15 minutes. Reduce oven temperature to 350° and bake for an additional 30 to 40 minutes, making sure quiche is set. Let quiche cool for 5 to 10 minutes before serving.

Bear Paw Inn... a B&B
Winter Park, Colorado

Asparagus Quiche

Makes 6 servings

10 stalks fresh asparagus, cooked and drained	**1 tsp. salt**
5 eggs, beaten	**2 T. fresh or 1 tsp. dried basil**
1 C. milk	**1 C. shredded Swiss cheese**

Preheat oven to 350°. Grease the bottom of a 10" pie pan. Place asparagus evenly over bottom of pie pan. In a large bowl, combine beaten eggs and milk. Add salt and basil and pour mixture over asparagus in pie pan. Cover with shredded Swiss cheese. Bake for 30 minutes, until quiche is set. Allow quiche to cool slightly before cutting and serving.

Elson Inn B&B
Magnolia, Ohio

Orange Omelet

Makes 4 servings

3 eggs, separated
Pinch of salt and pepper
1/2 T. butter
2 oranges

2 T. powdered sugar
2 1/2 T. orange juice
1 tsp. lemon juice

In a small bowl, combine egg yolks, salt, pepper and a little hot water. Beat until thick and lemon colored. Beat egg whites until stiff. Fold egg whites into egg yolk mixture, stirring until well blended. Butter the bottom and sides of an omelet pan. Pour mixture into pan, spreading evenly over bottom. Cook omelet over medium heat. When omelet is well "puffed" and delicately browned underneath, place pan on center grate of 350° oven to finish cooking the top. The omelet is done when it is firm to the touch. Peel oranges and cut or divide into sections. Sprinkle oranges with powdered sugar. Place 1/3 of oranges over omelet. Fold omelet and turn onto a hot platter. If desired, pour about 1 1/2 cups White Sauce over omelet. Place remaining sections of orange around omelet.

White Sauce

1 T. butter
1 T. flour
1/4 tsp. salt

Pinch of pepper
1 C. milk

In a small saucepan or double boiler, melt butter. In a small bowl, combine flour, salt and pepper. Using a wire whisk, stir flour mixture into butter until smooth and free of lumps. Gradually pour in milk, stirring constantly with a wire whisk. If not using a wire whisk, heat milk before adding to mixture to keep sauce smooth. Bring mixture to a boil. Boil for 2 minutes. Cook 15 minutes in double boiler. Stir well and pour over omelet.

B&B Associates Bay Colony
Boston, Massachusetts

Oven-Baked Omelet

Makes 4 servings

6 eggs
1/2 C. low-fat cottage
  cheese
1/2 C. sour cream
1/2 C. mild salsa

1 C. shredded Monterey
  Jack cheese
1 C. shredded Cheddar
  cheese

Preheat oven to 350°. Grease a 9" pie pan and set aside. In a medium bowl, whisk together eggs, cottage cheese and sour cream. Spread salsa over bottom of prepared pie pan. Sprinkle with shredded Monterey Jack and shredded Cheddar cheese. Pour egg mixture over cheese. Bake in oven for 45 minutes.

Parsonage on the Green B&B
Lee, Massachusetts

Baked Western Omelet

Makes 8 to 10 servings

8 slices bread, crust
  trimmed and reserved
1 1/2 C. shredded
  Cheddar cheese,
  divided
1/2 C. chopped green
  and red peppers,
  optional
1/2 C. chopped onion,
  optional
1/2 C. fresh sliced
  mushrooms

1/2 lb. julienne ham or
  cooked diced sausage,
  drained
8 eggs
2 C. milk
Salt and pepper to taste
1 to 2 T. yellow mustard,
  optional
4 T. butter or margarine

Preheat oven to 350°. Grease a 9x13" baking dish and arrange bread slices over bottom. Over bread, sprinkle 3/4 cup shredded Cheddar cheese, chopped green and red peppers, chopped onions, sliced mushrooms, diced ham or cooked sausage and remaining 3/4 cup shredded Cheddar cheese. In a separate bowl, combine eggs, milk, salt, pepper and mustard. Pour mixture slowly over ingredients in pan. Cube leftover bread crusts and toss with melted butter and arrange over top of omelet. Bake for 1 hour, until a knife inserted in the center comes out clean. This recipe can be prepared the night before by assembling all ingredients in a greased 9x13" baking dish, covering with plastic wrap and placing in refrigerator. Remove omelet casserole from refrigerator 1 hour prior to baking to avoid baking dish from cracking.

Lighthouse Valleyview B&B Inn
Dubuque, Iowa

French Toast Orange with Orange Sauce

Makes 6 servings

3 C. orange juice, divided
1/2 C. heavy cream
2 eggs
1 tsp. cinnamon
1/4 C. plus 2 T. sugar, divided
1/2 tsp. nutmeg
9 slices Texas toast
3 T. oil

3 T. butter
2 T. cornstarch
Pinch of salt
2 T. butter, melted
Powdered sugar for dusting
Fresh mint for garnish
1 sliced orange, reserve peel for garnish

In a large bowl, combine 1 cup orange juice, heavy cream, eggs, cinnamon, 1/4 cup sugar and nutmeg. Soak bread slices in mixture until saturated. In a large skillet, heat oil and butter. Fry bread slices in skillet on both sides until golden brown. Cut into triangles. In a small bowl, combine cornstarch with 1 teaspoon water, creating a paste. In a large saucepan, combine remaining 2 cups orange juice, 2 cups water, cornstarch paste, salt and remaining 2 tablespoons sugar. Heat over stovetop and add melted butter. Heat until sauce is a little thicker than syrup. Keep warm in double boiler until serving. To serve, place 3 French toast triangles on each plate. Pour 1 tablespoon sauce over toast and sprinkle with powdered sugar. Place mint and orange slices in center of French toast. Garnish with a twist of orange peel.

Nagle Warren Mansion B&B
Cheyenne, Wyoming

French Toast Stuffed with Bananas and Walnuts

Makes 4 servings

6 eggs
1/4 C. half n' half
1 tsp. vanilla
1/4 tsp. cinnamon
4 ripe bananas, peeled
   and mashed

1/4 C. coarsely
   chopped walnuts
1/8 tsp. nutmeg
8 slices egg bread
2 to 4 T. butter

In a medium bowl, beat eggs and stir in half n' half, vanilla and cinnamon. In a separate bowl, combine mashed bananas, chopped walnuts and nutmeg. Spread banana mixture generously onto 4 slices of egg bread and cover each slice with remaining 4 slices bread. In a medium saucepan, melt butter over medium heat. Dip sandwiches into egg mixture, turning until saturated on both sides. Place sandwiches into hot butter in saucepan and fry for about 2 minutes on each side. If desired, sprinkle with powdered sugar and garnish with walnut halves.

Amanda Gish House B&B
Elizabethtown, Pennsylvania

Caramelized French Toast
& Fried Apple Topping

Makes 6 servings

1/3 C. plus 4 T. butter, divided	5 eggs
1 C. plus 2 T. brown sugar, divided	1 1/2 C. milk
2 T. light corn syrup	1 tsp. cinnamon
6 slices French bread, cut 1" thick	2 T. sugar
	Pinch of salt
	6 C. peeled and sliced apples
	Powdered sugar for dusting

In a small saucepan, combine 1/3 cup butter, 1 cup brown sugar and light corn syrup. Cook over medium heat, stirring constantly, until butter melts. Pour brown sugar mixture into an ungreased 9x13" glass baking dish. Arrange the bread slices over the top of the brown sugar mixture and set aside. In a medium bowl, combine eggs, milk and cinnamon and pour over bread slices to saturate. Cover and refrigerate at least 2 hours or overnight. Preheat oven to 350°. Uncover bread and bake for 30 to 35 minutes, until lightly browned and center is set. Meanwhile, in a medium saucepan, melt remaining 4 tablespoons butter over medium heat. Add sugar, remaining 2 tablespoons brown sugar and salt. Add sliced apples and fry over medium heat until fully cooked. Remove French toast from oven and let stand for 10 minutes. Top French toast with fried apples and dust with powdered sugar.

Autumn Pond B&B
Leavenworth, Washington

Homespun Farm French Toast

1 C. pecans
8 T. butter
1 C. brown sugar
2 T. light or dark
   corn syrup
Sweet bread slices,
   sliced 3/4" thick

5 eggs
1 1/2 C. half n' half
1 tsp. vanilla
1/4 tsp. salt

In a greased 9x13" baking dish, spread pecans evenly over bottom. In a medium saucepan over low medium heat, melt butter, brown sugar and corn syrup. Once melted, pour mixture evenly over pecans in baking dish. Fit slices of bread tightly over pecans. In a separate bowl, beat eggs, half n' half, vanilla and salt. Mix well and pour over bread slices in pan. Cover pan and chill in refrigerator for at least 8 hours. Preheat oven to 350°. Bake French toast in oven for 35 to 40 minutes. Remove pan from oven and let cool 2 to 3 minutes. Flip pan upside down on a baking sheet and then flip back into pan. This is to ensure that the French toast won't stick to the pan. Cut into pieces and serve.

Homespun Farm B&B
Griswold, Connecticut

54

Caramel French Toast

1/2 C. butter	1 1/2 C. milk
1 C. brown sugar	1 tsp. vanilla
1 loaf French bread	2 T. sugar
5 eggs	1/4 tsp. salt

In a small saucepan, combine butter and brown sugar. Simmer over medium heat until mixture becomes syrupy. Pour over bottom of a 9x13" glass baking dish. Slice French bread into 3/4" thick slices and remove crusts. Place slices over syrup mixture in dish. In a large bowl, beat eggs, milk, vanilla, sugar and salt. Pour over bread. Cover and refrigerate overnight. Preheat oven to 350°. Bake, uncovered, for 35 minutes.

Sunrise Farm B&B
Salem, South Carolina

55

Overnight Apple French Toast

Makes 9 servings

1 C. brown sugar
1/2 C. butter or
   margarine
2 T. light corn syrup
2 large tart apples,
   peeled and sliced
   1/4" thick
3 eggs

1 C. milk
1 tsp. vanilla
9 slices day old French
   bread, cut 3/4" thick
1 C. applesauce
1 (10 oz.) jar apple jelly
1/2 tsp. cinnamon
1/8 tsp. ground cloves

In a small saucepan over medium heat, combine brown sugar, butter and corn syrup. Cook for 5 to 7 minutes, until thickened. Pour mixture into an ungreased 9x13" baking dish. Arrange apple slices over mixture in baking dish. In a medium bowl, combine eggs, milk and vanilla, until well mixed. Dip bread slices into egg mixture, letting soak for 1 minute. Place bread slices over apples in pan. Cover and refrigerate overnight. Remove pan from refrigerator 30 minutes before baking. Preheat oven to 350°. Bake, uncovered, for 35 to 40 minutes. In a medium saucepan over medium heat, combine applesauce, apple jelly, cinnamon and ground cloves. Cook until thoroughly heated. To serve, place French toast on serving plates and cover with hot applesauce mixture.

Deacon Timothy Pratt B&B
Old Saybrook, Connecticut

Coconut Praline French Toast

Makes 6 to 8 servings

6 large eggs	**1 C. shredded coconut**
1 C. milk	**1/2 C. chopped pecans**
1/2 C. French vanilla	**12 to 16 slices French**
flavored creamer	**bread, cut 3/4" thick**
Dash of salt	

In a large bowl, combine eggs, milk, French vanilla creamer and salt, mixing until frothy. On a tray, spread shredded coconut and pecans evenly. Dip slices of bread in egg mixture until saturated. Roll bread slices on tray to coat with coconut and pecan mixture. Grease and preheat a griddle to medium heat. Place coated bread slices on a well oiled griddle, cooking until coconut is golden brown. Turn slices carefully, adjusting heat to avoid coconut from burning. Serve immediately or place finished French toast on a baking sheet and keep warm in a 200° oven for up to 30 minutes. If desired, serve with warmed maple syrup.

Variation
Substitute 1 tablespoon vanilla extract mixed with 1/2 cup milk or cream for French vanilla creamer.

Lighthouse Valleyview B&B Inn
Dubuque, Iowa

Pancakes á la Aubrey: Buckwheat Pancakes with Crunchy Chocolate Peanut Butter Sauce

Makes about 12 pancakes

2 T. butter
1/4 C. maple syrup
2 T. crunchy peanut
    butter
1 to 2 tsp. chocolate
    chips
1 C. flour
1/2 C. buckwheat flour

3/4 C. old fashioned or
    quick oats
1/4 C. flaxseed meal
2 T. baking powder
1 egg, beaten
3 T. vegetable oil
1 1/2 to 2 1/2 C. milk

To make crunchy chocolate peanut butter sauce, combine butter, maple syrup, crunchy peanut butter and chocolate chips in a medium saucepan. Warm over low heat, stirring often, until mixture is liquefied. Set aside, keeping warm over low heat. Preheat griddle to 375°. In a large bowl, combine flour, buckwheat flour, oats, flaxseed meal and baking powder. Add beaten egg, vegetable oil and milk. Stir until mixture is uniformly mixed. Batter should pour slowly. Drop batter in 1/4 cup amounts and cook for about 1 minute and 45 seconds per side, until golden brown. Place pancakes on serving plate and serve with warm crunchy chocolate peanut butter sauce. If desired, pancakes can be served with other sauces such as maple or blueberry syrup.

Sassafras Ridge B&B
Carbondale, Illinois

Swedish Lemon Pancakes

Makes 4 servings

1 1/2 C. flour	2 1/2 C. milk
3 T. sugar	1 tsp. vanilla
1/2 tsp. salt	3 T. butter
Zest of 2 lemons,	Powdered sugar
divided	Sweetened sour cream*
3 eggs	

In a large bowl, whisk together flour, sugar, salt and half of the lemon zest. In a separate bowl, beat eggs, milk and vanilla together. Pour egg mixture into flour mixture and mix until smooth. Butter the bottom of a 10" non-stick skillet and heat over medium high heat until butter just begins to brown. Pour approximately 1/3 cup batter into hot pan and swirl to coat bottom. Cook until bottom side is lightly browned and flip to cook other side. Transfer to a plate and keep warm while cooking remaining batter. Spread fresh berries, peaches, jams or brown sugar over pancakes. To serve, roll up pancakes, with filling inside, and dust generously with powdered sugar. Garnish with remaining half of lemon zest and sweetened sour cream.

* To make sweetened sour cream, combine 1 cup whipping cream, 1/2 cup sour cream and 2 tablespoons brown sugar. Whip into stiff peaks.

Autumn Pond B&B
Leavenworth, Washington

Bear Paw Buttermilk Pancakes with Blueberry Compote

1 1/4 C. flour
1/3 C. plus 2 T. sugar, divided
1 tsp. baking powder
1 tsp. baking soda
1/2 tsp. salt
1 C. buttermilk
1 C. sour cream
1 egg
2 tsp. vanilla
3 T. unsalted butter
2 1/2 C. fresh or frozen blueberries, divided
1/3 C. water

In a large bowl, whisk together flour, 2 tablespoons sugar, baking powder, baking soda and salt. In a separate bowl, whisk together buttermilk, sour cream, egg and vanilla. Add buttermilk mixture to dry ingredients. Stir together until mixture forms a batter that is just blended and still lumpy. On a griddle over medium heat, melt butter. Pour 1/3 cup batter onto griddle to make each pancake, spacing pancakes 2" apart. Cook pancakes until bubbles break on the surface, about 3 to 4 minutes. Turn pancakes and cook until bottoms are golden brown, another 3 to 4 minutes. Keep pancakes warm. To make blueberry compote, in a small saucepan over medium heat, combine 1 1/2 cups blueberries, remaining 1/3 cup sugar and water. Simmer, stirring often, over heat until blueberries burst, about 10 minutes. Add remaining 1 cup blueberries and cook until compote coats the back of a spoon, about 8 minutes. To serve, pour blueberry compote and butter over warm pancakes.

Note
Blueberry compote can be made up to 3 days in advance. After cooking berries, cover and chill in refrigerator.

Bear Paw Inn... a B&B
Winter Park, Colorado

Caramel Apple Pancakes

Makes 6 servings

3 T. butter	1 1/2 C. whole milk
5 T. lemon juice	Pinch of nutmeg
1 C. sugar	1/2 tsp. vanilla
1 1/2 tsp. cinnamon	Pinch of salt
6 C. diced apples	Caramel sauce
1 1/2 C. flour, sifted	Powdered sugar
6 eggs	

Preheat oven to 425°. Place frying pans in oven to heat. In a medium saucepan over medium heat, combine butter and lemon juice. In a small bowl, combine sugar and cinnamon. Mix well and pour into saucepan. Add diced apples to saucepan and mix all together. Bring to a boil, cover and reduce heat to low, stirring every 5 minutes. When apples are hot, keep covered and remove from heat. In a medium bowl, combine sifted flour, eggs, whole milk, nutmeg, vanilla and salt. Mix well. Lightly grease the heated frying pans and add 1/2 cup batter to hot pan. Bake in oven for 11 minutes, making sure not to open oven during cooking time. Remove frying pans from oven and place pancake on a plate. Cover half of the pancake with hot apple mixture and drizzle with caramel sauce. Fold empty half of pancake over apple-filled side. Dust pancake with powdered sugar and drizzle more caramel sauce over pancake and onto plate. Repeat with remaining batter and apple filling.

Martha's Vineyard B&B
South Haven, Michigan

Pumpkin Pancakes

Makes 10 pancakes

1 1/2 C. flour
1 tsp. baking powder
1 1/2 tsp. pumpkin pie
   spice
1/4 tsp. baking soda

1/4 tsp. salt
1 egg
1/4 C. canned pumpkin
1 1/2 C. milk
3 T. cooking oil

In a medium bowl, combine flour, baking powder, pumpkin pie spice, baking soda and salt. In a separate bowl, beat together egg, canned pumpkin, milk and oil. Add flour mixture to milk mixture, stirring until just blended but still lumpy. Pour about 1/4 cup batter for each pancake on a hot greased griddle or heavy skillet. Cook over medium heat until browned, turning to cook both sides of pancake.

Sunrise Farm B&B
Salem, South Carolina

Atwood Dutch Eggs

Makes 1 serving

3 T. butter, divided	2 eggs, divided
1/2 C. flour, divided	1/8 tsp. salt
1 3/4 C. milk, divided	Salt and pepper to taste
5 to 6 oz. American cheese, cubed	2 slices bacon, cooked and crumbled

Preheat oven to 475°. In a double boiler, melt 2 tablespoons butter. When butter comes to a boil, add 1/4 cup flour and immediately stir with a whisk. Add 1 1/2 cups milk, continuing to stir. Return to a boil. When sauce thickens, remove from heat. Add cubed cheese, stirring until melted. In a blender, combine 1 egg, remaining 1/4 cup milk, remaining 1/4 cup flour and salt, mixing to form a batter. Grease a 6" soufflé dish and place remaining 1 tablespoon butter in dish. Place in oven for 3 to 4 minutes, until butter is completely melted. Remove soufflé dish and pour in batter. Bake for 12 minutes. Place remaining egg in a small greased custard dish and top with salt and pepper. Add egg to oven for final 10 minutes baking time. As the batter cooks, it will rise, forming a pocket in the center. Remove pancake from the soufflé dish, top side up. Insert most of the crumbled bacon into the pocket. Insert egg into pocket. Top with warm cheese sauce. Garnish with remaining crumbled bacon and serve immediately.

Atwood House B&B
Lincoln, Nebraska

"Feather Bed" Eggs

Makes 6 servings

6 slices bread, cut thick	**1 1/2 C. whole milk**
Butter	**6 eggs**
Pepper to taste	**Dried oregano to taste**
1 1/2 C. shredded white Cheddar cheese, or any kind, divided	

Grease 6 small ramekins. Butter 1 side of each slice of bread. Stuff 1 slice of bread, buttered side up, into each ramekin. Generously pepper each slice of bread. Sprinkle each slice with 1/4 cup cheese. In a medium bowl, beat milk with eggs and dried oregano. Pour an equal amount of egg mixture over cheese and bread in each ramekin. Cover and refrigerate overnight. Uncover and place ramekins in cold oven. Bake at 350° for 30 to 40 minutes, until puffed and golden brown. Remove eggs from ramekins and serve immediately.

Variation
Use a 9x13" baking dish instead of individual ramekins, arranging bread along bottom of baking dish. May add diced ham, sausage, onions, green peppers or mushrooms. Place these ingredients on top of bread, but under cheese, prior to covering with egg mixture.

Highland Lake Inn, B&B
East Andover, New Hampshire

Eggs Florentine

1 pkg. chopped spinach   **8 oz. shredded Swiss cheese**
8 eggs   **8 oz. crumbled feta cheese**
1/2 C. butter, melted   **1/8 tsp. nutmeg**

Preheat oven to 350°. Cook spinach according to package directions. Drain well and spread spinach over paper towels. Squeeze spinach in paper towels until all water is removed. Set aside. In a medium bowl, beat eggs and add melted butter, shredded Swiss cheese, feta cheese and nutmeg. Add spinach and mix until thoroughly blended. Pour into a greased 9x12" baking dish. Bake for 30 minutes. Cut into squares and serve.

Aleksander House B&B
Louisville, Kentucky

Southwest Eggs Benedict

Makes 4 servings

4 English muffins
1/2 C. grated Parmesan
  cheese
1 T. butter
1 T. flour
1/4 tsp. salt
1/4 tsp. pepper
1 C. half n' half
1 egg yolk, beaten

1 C. shredded pepper
  Jack cheese
1/2 C. diced green chilies
8 slices smoked turkey
8 eggs, poached
1/2 C. diced tomatoes
1/2 C. finely sliced green
  onions

Split each English muffin and toast lightly. Butter and sprinkle each half with Parmesan cheese and keep warm. To make cheese sauce, in a 1-quart saucepan, melt 1 tablespoon butter. Stir in flour, salt and pepper and cook until foamy and cream colored. Whisk in half n' half and heat until slightly thickened. In a small bowl, whisk together egg yolk and 1/2 cup of the liquid mixture. Whisk egg yolk mixture back into liquid mixture in saucepan. Cook sauce until slightly thickened and stir in shredded pepper Jack cheese and diced green chilies. Set aside. To serve, place 2 muffin halves on each plate. Top each muffin with a slice of smoked turkey and a poached egg. Pour 1/4 cup cheese sauce over each egg and sprinkle with diced tomatoes and green onions.

Autumn Pond B&B
Leavenworth, Washington

Creamy Scrambled Eggs

8 eggs
1/4 C. whole milk
1/4 tsp. salt
1/4 tsp. pepper
3 T. fresh chopped
   chives, divided

1 T. butter
4 oz. cream cheese, cut
   into cubes
Fresh chive sprigs and
   chive blossoms for
   garnish, optional

In a large bowl, beat eggs, milk, salt, pepper and 1 tablespoon chopped chives. In a large non-stick pan, melt butter over medium heat. Add egg mixture and cook like standard scrambled eggs. When eggs are about half set, add cubes of cream cheese. The cream cheese should melt by the time the eggs are finished cooking. Divide eggs onto serving plates and sprinkle remaining 2 tablespoons chopped chives around the perimeter of the plates. If desired, add fresh chive sprigs and chive blossoms for garnish.

Inn at Valley Farms B&B and Cottages
Walpole, New Hampshire

Eggs Callahan

1 (16 to 18 oz.) pkg. frozen shredded hash browns, thawed
1/2 C. butter
2 C. shredded Cheddar cheese
1/2 lb. cooked sausage, sliced or crumbled
2 1/2 C. diced mushrooms
1 C. sliced yellow pepper
1 C. sliced red pepper
5 eggs
1/2 C. milk
Salt and pepper to taste

Preheat oven to 450°. Press thawed hash browns between paper towels to remove moisture. Grease a deep quiche pan and press hash browns into pan, forming a crust. Brush hash browns with butter and bake for 30 minutes. Remove from oven. Reduce oven temperature to 350°. Sprinkle shredded Cheddar cheese over hash browns. Add cooked sausage, diced mushrooms, sliced yellow peppers and sliced red peppers. In a medium bowl, beat eggs and milk thoroughly. Add salt and pepper, or other seasonings, to taste. Pour egg mixture over ingredients in quiche pan. Bake for 40 minutes, until eggs are fully cooked. Slice and, if desired, serve with slices of tomato, avocado or salsa on the side.

Bear Paw Inn... a B&B
Winter Park, Colorado

Sausage and Egg Bake

Makes 12 servings

1 lb. bulk pork sausage, cooked and drained

1 1/2 C. sliced mushrooms

8 medium green onions, sliced

2 medium tomatoes, chopped

2 C. shredded mozzarella cheese

1 1/4 C. Bisquick baking mix

1 C. milk

1 1/2 tsp. salt

1/2 tsp. pepper

1 1/2 tsp. fresh chopped oregano (or 1/2 tsp. dried oregano)

12 eggs

Preheat oven to 350°. Grease a 9x13" baking dish. Layer sausage, mushrooms, onions, tomatoes and mozzarella cheese in prepared baking dish. In a medium bowl, whisk together Bisquick, milk, salt, pepper, oregano and eggs. Pour Bisquick mixture over ingredients in baking dish. Bake for about 30 to 35 minutes, until golden brown and set.

Sheep Hill B&B and Antique Shop
East Earl, Pennsylvania

Chilies Rellenos Bake

Makes 8 to 10 servings

8 eggs
1 C. sour cream
1/4 tsp. salt
2 drops red pepper
    sauce
2 C. shredded Cheddar
    cheese

2 C. shredded Monterey
    Jack cheese
2 (4 oz.) cans chopped
    green chilies in juice
Salsa

Preheat oven to 350°. Grease a 9x13" baking dish and set aside. In a large bowl, beat eggs, sour cream, salt and red pepper sauce with a wire whisk. Stir in shredded Cheddar cheese, shredded Monterey Jack and chopped chilies in juice. Pour mixture into prepared baking dish. Bake, uncovered, for 45 minutes, until golden brown. Remove from oven and let sit 5 minutes before cutting into servings. Serve with salsa.

Variation
To make individual servings, mixture can be poured into 10 small tart pans and baked for 35 minutes.

Atwood House B&B
Lincoln, Nebraska

70

Spinach Frittata

Makes 12 to 14 servings

1/4 pkg. frozen chopped spinach, thawed and drained 1 large zucchini, grated	1/2 lb. shredded Monterey Jack cheese 1 C. grated Parmesan cheese 16 to 18 eggs

Preheat oven to 375°. In a large bowl, combine thawed and drained chopped spinach, grated zucchini, shredded Monterey Jack cheese, grated Parmesan cheese and eggs. Mix well. Pour mixture to fill individual greased ramekins 3/4 full. Bake for 25 minutes.

Packard House B&B
Mendocino, California

71

Breakfast Pie

5 eggs
1/2 C. milk
1/2 tsp. salt
1/4 tsp. pepper
3/4 C. shredded
   Monterey Jack cheese

1 1/4 C. shredded Cheddar
   cheese, divided
2 C. shredded potatoes
1/2 C. cooked ham,
   bacon or sausage
1 T. dried parsley flakes

Preheat oven to 350°. In a large bowl, whisk together eggs, milk, salt and pepper. Stir in shredded Monterey Jack cheese and 3/4 cup shredded Cheddar cheese and set aside. Grease a 9" pie pan. In a separate bowl, toss together shredded potatoes and remaining 1/2 cup shredded Cheddar cheese. Press potato mixture into prepared pie pan to form a crust. Sprinkle cooked meat over crust. Pour egg mixture over meat. Sprinkle parsley flakes over pie. Bake for 35 to 40 minutes, until pie is set. Serve hot or reheat in microwave before serving.

The Dominion House B&B
Blooming Grove, New York

Spanish Breakfast Basket

4 T. butter, divided
3/4 C. flour
3/4 C. milk
1/2 tsp. salt
1/2 tsp. pepper
1/2 tsp. dried oregano
1/2 tsp. garlic powder

1/2 tsp. onion powder
1/4 tsp. paprika
5 to 6 C. frozen shredded
    hash browns, cooked
6 slices bacon, cooked and
    crumbled, optional

Preheat oven to 400°. Place two 8" round pans in oven with 2 tablespoons butter in each pan. Rotate pans until butter is melted and coats sides of pans. In a large bowl, combine flour, milk, salt, pepper, dried oregano, garlic powder, onion powder and paprika. Beat mixture until smooth and divide batter evenly between the two heated pans. Bake for 20 to 25 minutes, until golden brown. Immediately remove from oven and fill baked basket with cooked hash browns. If desired, garnish with crumbled bacon. Serve immediately.

Frog Hollow B&B
Lexington, Virginia

Sunday Morning

Makes 12 servings

9 eggs
1 lb. Jimmy Dean sage
sausage, cooked and
crumbled
3 C. whole milk
3 slices white bread,
crusts removed and
cut into 1" cubes

1 1/2 C. shredded cheese,
any kind
1 T. dried parsley flakes
1/4 tsp. pepper
1/2 tsp. salt

Generously grease a 9x13" baking dish. In greased baking dish, combine eggs, crumbled sausage, whole milk, bread cubes, shredded cheese, parsley flakes, pepper and salt. Cover with plastic wrap and chill in refrigerator overnight. Preheat oven to 350°. Bake for 1 hour, until set. Cut into squares. If desired, ingredients can be combined in a large bowl and spooned into individual greased ramekins. Set ramekins on a baking sheet and bake in a 350° oven for 1 hour.

Martha's Vineyard B&B
South Haven, Michigan

Cheesy Apple-Bacon Casserole

Makes 8 to 10 servings

1 apple, peeled, cored
and diced
2 T. sugar
1 1/2 C. Bisquick baking
mix
1 1/2 C. milk

4 eggs
2 C. shredded Cheddar
cheese
1 lb. bacon, cooked and
crumbled

Preheat oven to 375°. Grease a 9x13" baking dish. In a medium bowl, mix diced apples and sugar. Spread apple mixture into bottom of prepared baking dish. In a medium bowl, combine Bisquick, milk and eggs. Pour over apples in baking dish. Sprinkle with shredded Cheddar cheese and crumbled bacon. Bake for 30 to 35 minutes, until knife inserted in center of casserole comes out clean.

Sheep Hill B&B and Antique Shop
East Earl, Pennsylvania

High Noon Huevos Rancheros

Makes 4 servings

1 can black beans, drained

1 (15 oz.) can refried beans

1 can green chilies, drained

1 jar salsa

3/4 to 1 lb. Jimmy Dean pork sausage, cooked and crumbled

4 flour tortillas

8 eggs

Butter

1 1/2 C. shredded Monterey Jack cheese

1 1/2 C. shredded Cheddar cheese

Sour cream

2 green onions, finely chopped

Fresh chopped cilantro to garnish

In separate bowls, microwave drained black beans, refried beans, green chilies and salsa for 1 minute each. If the cooked sausage is not warm, microwave for 1 minute, as well. Wrap tortillas in foil and place in oven for 15 minutes to warm. In a medium pan or skillet, fry eggs in butter, 2 at a time. While eggs are frying, spread warmed refried beans to within 1/4" of the edge of each tortilla. Divide crumbled sausage evenly over tortillas. Divide warmed black beans and chilies evenly over tortillas. Place 2 fried eggs over each tortilla and dab each tortilla with warmed salsa. Divide Monterey Jack and Cheddar cheeses evenly over tortillas. Place tortillas under broiler until cheese is melted. Top each tortilla with sour cream and chopped green onions. Garnish with fresh chopped cilantro.

Bear Paw Inn... a B&B
Winter Park, Colorado

The Deacon's Egg Casserole

Makes 6 to 8 servings

**1 pkg. breakfast sausage
   links
6 slices Challah bread,
   cut into small cubes
1 tsp. dried thyme
1/2 pkg. fresh baby spinach**

**12 eggs
2 C. whole milk
1 T. fresh chopped dill
1 1/2 C. grated Parmesan
   or Romano cheese**

Preheat oven to 350°. In a microwave-safe dish, cook sausage in microwave for 2 minutes, until heated throughout. Drain sausage and cut into small pieces. Grease a 9" square baking dish. Place bread cubes in an even layer over bottom of baking dish. Sprinkle dried thyme and cut sausage over bread cubes in pan. Cover with a generous layer of baby spinach. In a large bowl, combine eggs and milk, just until blended. Pour mixture over ingredients in pan, filling pan 2/3 full. With the back of a spoon, lightly press down on mixture and let sit for 10 minutes. Sprinkle chopped dill over ingredients in pan and top with grated cheese. Cover with aluminum foil. Bake for 45 minutes, until set. Remove aluminum foil and cook for an additional 5 minutes. Cut and serve immediately. If desired, freeze individual squares wrapped in plastic wrap and aluminum foil and microwave to reheat.

*Deacon Timothy Pratt B&B
Old Saybrook, Connecticut*

Potato & Mushroom Frittata

Makes 12 to 14 servings

1 large onion, diced
1 lb. Crimini
   mushrooms, or any
   kind, diced
Olive oil
Butter

1 lb. frozen hash browns
16 to 18 eggs
1 C. grated Parmesan
   cheese
1 1/2 C. shredded Monterey
   Jack cheese

Preheat oven to 375°. In a large skillet over medium heat, sauté onions and mushrooms in olive oil and butter, until onions have caramelized. Add frozen hash browns and mix well. If needed, add more olive oil or butter and cook until hash browns are tender. Let cool. In a large bowl, beat eggs. Add grated Parmesan cheese and shredded Monterey Jack cheese. Fold cooked potato and onion mixture into egg mixture. Pour mixture to fill individual greased ramekins to 3/4 full. Bake for 25 minutes.

Packard House B&B
Mendocino, California

Southwest Layered Tortillas

Makes 3 hearty servings

1/2 C. corn oil
6 flour tortillas
6 large eggs
1/4 C. heavy cream or
   half n' half
1/2 C. Pico de Gallo or
   salsa
1/4 C. finely chopped
   cilantro, divided

1/4 C. chopped scallions
2 C. shredded Cheddar
   cheese, divided
Salt and pepper to taste
3 C. refried beans
Jalapenos for garnish

In a large frying pan, heat corn oil. When oil is hot, fry tortillas on both sides, one at a time, just until slightly brown and puffy. Drain tortillas on paper towels and place in a 200° oven to keep warm. In a large bowl, beat eggs and cream. Add Pico de Gallo or salsa, 1/8 cup chopped cilantro, scallions and 1/2 cup shredded Cheddar cheese. Stir until well mixed. Drain oil from frying pan, leaving some oil to coat the pan. Add egg mixture to frying pan and cook over medium heat until eggs are barely cooked. Add salt and pepper. Meanwhile, heat refried beans. If using canned beans, add a little water and heat beans in a medium pan over high heat until beans are smooth. Beans can be heated in a microwave with 2 1/2 cups water for 5 minutes. To prepare tortillas, place 1 tortilla on each of 3 plates and spread 1/3 of the egg mixture over each tortilla. Sprinkle 1/4 cup Cheddar cheese over each tortilla. Place another tortilla over cheese and spread 1 cup of refried beans over each. Sprinkle tortillas with remaining 3/4 cup cheese. Garnish with remaining 1/8 cup cilantro and jalapenos. If desired, serve with salsa, sour cream, guacamole or hot sauce on the side.

La Paz in Desert Springs B&B
Scottsdale, Arizona

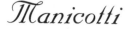Manicotti

8 eggs, room
   temperature, divided
1 1/2 C. flour, sifted
1/4 tsp. salt
1 1/2 C. water
3 lbs. ricotta cheese

1 C. shredded mozzarella
   cheese
1 C. grated Parmesan cheese
Salt and pepper to taste
4 to 5 C. tomato sauce, any
   kind

In a large bowl, combine 6 eggs, sifted flour, salt and water. Lightly grease a hot skillet. Add 3 tablespoons of the mixture at a time, moving skillet from side to side to cover bottom like a crepe. Be careful not to let batter brown and do not turn over. Once top of batter is dry, remove from skillet and repeat until all batter is used. Let cool. Preheat oven to 350°. To make filling, in a large bowl, combine ricotta cheese, shredded mozzarella cheese, grated Parmesan cheese, salt and pepper. Fill each crepe with cheese mixture by spreading a little down the center of each. Roll up and place, seam side down, in a 9x12" pan. Cover with tomato sauce and bake for 30 to 45 minutes.

Cocalico Creek B&B
Denver, Pennsylvania

Luncheon Chicken Salad

6 C. cooked chopped
   chicken
2 C. mayonnaise
1/4 C. Dijon mustard
2 C. pineapple tidbits,
   drained

2 C. diced apples
1 1/2 tsp. salt
2 C. thinly sliced celery
3/4 C. cashew halves,
   optional

In a large bowl, combine cooked chopped chicken, mayonnaise and mustard. Mix well and add drained pineapple tidbits, diced apples, salt and sliced celery. If desired, add cashews as garnish before serving.

Big Moose Inn B&B
Eagle Bay, New York

Chicken & Rice Hot Dish

1 C. instant rice
2 to 4 C. fresh chopped
   chicken
1 can cream of
   mushroom soup

1 can cream of
   chicken soup
1 C. milk
1 pkg. dry onion soup
   mix

Preheat oven to 350°. Grease a 9x13" baking dish. Spread instant rice evenly over bottom of dish and lay chopped chicken, skin side up, over rice. In a medium bowl, combine cream of mushroom soup, cream of chicken soup and milk. Mix until evenly blended and pour over chicken in dish. Sprinkle onion soup mix over chicken in dish. Bake for 1 1/2 to 2 hours, depending on size of chicken pieces.

Calmar Guesthouse B&B
Calmar, Iowa

Baked Apple Sausage Loaf

Makes 14 servings

2 eggs, lightly beaten	1 C. diced apples
1/2 C. milk	1/4 C. chopped onions
1 1/2 C. crushed Ritz	1/4 tsp. white pepper
crackers	2 lbs. breakfast sausage

Preheat oven to 350°. Lightly grease a ring mold or bundt pan and set aside. In a large bowl, beat together eggs and milk. Add crushed crackers and let stand for a few minutes until all liquid is absorbed. Add diced apples, chopped onions, white pepper and sausage. Mix well with hands and pat mixture into prepared mold or bundt pan. Cover a baking sheet with aluminum foil. Place on baking sheet and bake for 1 hour. Drain excess grease onto paper towels. Invert loaf onto serving dish. Serve immediately or let cool slightly, cover with plastic wrap and refrigerate until needed. To prepare leftovers, slice loaf into 1" slices. Place slices on baking sheet covered with aluminum foil. Bake in a 350° oven for about 30 minutes, turning once.

Rock Cottage Gardens... a Bed & Breakfast Inn
Eureka Springs, Arkansas

Crab Stir Fry
with Peanut Sauce

2 tsp. olive oil
1 pkg. fresh or frozen
　stir fry vegetables
2 tsp. minced gingerroot
　or ground ginger,
　divided
2 tsp. minced garlic or
　garlic powder, divided
1 (8 oz.) pkg. Louis Kemp
　crab delights

1/2 C. crunchy peanut
　butter
1/3 C. white vinegar
1/2 C. sugar
3 T. soy sauce
1 T. olive, sesame or
　vegetable oil
2 T. water

In a large skillet over medium high heat, heat olive oil. Sauté stir fry vegetables, 1 teaspoon ginger and 1 teaspoon garlic. Add crabmeat and stir until heated throughout. To make peanut sauce, in a medium bowl, whisk together peanut butter, vinegar, sugar, soy sauce, oil, remaining 1 teaspoon garlic, remaining 1 teaspoon ginger and water. Mix until smooth and pour over stir fry. If desired, serve with rice. Peanut sauce can be made ahead of time and stored in refrigerator.

Canyon Road Inn B&B
Turtle Lake, Wisconsin

Steak Continental

2 lbs. flank steak
1 clove garlic, minced
3/4 T. salt
2 to 3 T. soy sauce

1 T. tomato paste
1 T. salad oil
1/2 tsp. pepper
1/2 T. dried oregano

Score both sides of steak by cutting 1/4" deep diagonal slices, forming diamond-shaped cuts. In a medium bowl, mix minced garlic with salt. Add soy sauce, tomato paste, oil, pepper and oregano. Mix well and rub mixture into both sides of steaks. Wrap steaks with waxed paper and chill in refrigerator for 5 to 6 hours or overnight. To cook steaks, place in broiler for 5 to 8 minutes on each side, or to desired doneness.

Note
This rub can be used on tenderloins or other meats and cooked over a grill.

Big Moose Inn B&B
Eagle Bay, New York

85

Shrimp Waterloo

Makes 2 servings

8 to 10 large shrimp
Lemon juice
Salt and pepper
2 T. oil
1/4 C. plus 3 T.
   butter, divided
1/4 C. dry vermouth

1 or 2 cloves garlic,
   crushed
Fresh chopped parsley
Fresh chopped dill or
   thyme, optional
1/2 C. white wine

Sprinkle shrimp with lemon juice, salt and pepper to taste. In a medium saucepan over medium high heat, heat oil and 2 tablespoons butter. Add seasoned shrimp to saucepan and sauté on both sides, until pink. Add dry vermouth to saucepan and ignite with a kitchen torch. Flambé shrimp and remove shrimp from saucepan after flame has died. Add 1 tablespoon butter and sauté crushed garlic and chopped parsley. If desired, sauté chopped dill or thyme in saucepan. Pour in white wine and a dash of lemon juice and simmer until liquid reduces by half. Stir in remaining 1/4 cup butter and add salt and pepper to taste. Return shrimp to pan, being careful not to boil. To serve, place sauce on serving plates and arrange shrimp over sauce. Delicious when served with rice and asparagus.

Waterloo Country Inn
Princess Anne, Maryland

The Cliff House Seafood Crepes

1 C. milk
1 C. plus 4 T. flour, divided
2 eggs
1 egg white
Pinch of salt
5 T. butter, divided
1 to 2 green onions,
   chopped
6 to 8 mushrooms, chopped
1 tsp. Oregon Favor
   lemon larkin spice

4 C. heavy whipping
   cream, divided
1 C. shredded Monterey
   Jack cheese
1 C. ricotta cheese
1 C. flaked crabmeat
1/2 C. baby shrimp, drained
1/2 C. grated Parmesan
   cheese
3 to 4 small tomatoes,
   chopped

Preheat oven to 350°. In a blender, puree milk, 1 cup flour, eggs, egg white and salt for 1 minute. Heat a crepe pan over medium heat. Cover bottom of hot pan with 1/4 cup of batter. Cook quickly, until edges of batter come loose from sides of pan. Flip crepe, cooking other side for a few seconds. Remove crepe from pan and repeat with remaining batter. Set aside crepes to cool. In a small saucepan over medium heat, melt 1 tablespoon butter. Add onions and mushrooms, cooking until mushrooms are tender. Mix in lemon larkin spice, remove from heat and set aside. In a separate saucepan over medium heat, melt 4 tablespoons butter. Gradually add 4 tablespoons flour to melted butter, until mixture is the consistency of gravy. Mix in 2 cups cream, stirring until thickened. Mix in Monterey Jack and ricotta cheese, stirring until melted. In a medium bowl, combine half of the cheese mixture, crabmeat and shrimp. Stir in mushroom mixture, mixing until just blended. To assemble, place about 1/4 cup seafood mixture over each crepe. Secure crepes by folding edges like an envelope. In a large saucepan, fry filled crepes in melted butter, until slightly browned. Place crepes in a baking dish. Bake for 30 minutes. To remaining melted cheese mixture, add 2 cups cream and Parmesan cheese. Cook over medium heat, stirring frequently, until mixture almost reaches boiling point. To serve, place 1 crepe on each plate and top with 1 tablespoon tomatoes. Spoon about 1/4 cup cheese sauce over each crepe.

Cliff House B&B
Waldport, Oregon

Shrimp Scampi Rockefeller

Makes 2 servings

1/2 lb. large shrimp, shelled
1 pkg. stuffing, cooked
4 T. butter, melted
2 tsp. paprika
6 cloves garlic, minced
1 bunch green onions, chopped
1 T. olive oil

1/2 (10 oz.) pkg. fresh baby spinach leaves
1/2 C. coarsely chopped basil leaves
1/2 tsp. Tabasco sauce
1/2 to 1 tsp. white wine vinegar
Salt and pepper
3 T. Pernod anise-flavored liqueur

Preheat oven to 375°. Grease a large baking dish and set aside. Butterfly shrimp by cutting almost completely through lengthwise along inside curve. Split open shrimp and devein. Place opened shrimp in prepared baking dish. Mound 2 tablespoons cooked stuffing onto each shrimp, pressing down gently. Pour melted butter over shrimp and sprinkle with paprika. Bake for 20 minutes, until golden brown. Meanwhile, in a heavy skillet over medium high heat, sauté minced garlic and green onions in olive oil until softened, about 2 minutes. Add spinach to skillet and cook until tender and wilted, stirring occasionally. Mix in chopped basil leaves, Tabasco sauce, vinegar, salt and pepper. Remove from heat and mix in liqueur. Spoon spinach mixture over shrimp and bake until shrimp are just cooked through, about another 8 minutes.

Big Moose Inn B&B
Eagle Bay, New York

Orange Chicken on Rice

1 pkg. uncooked white
    rice
1 pkg. uncooked wild
    rice
2 C. cooked chopped
    chicken
1 to 2 T. butter

1 C. cold water
1 T. cornstarch
1 C. orange marmalade
Salt to taste
1 to 2 C. frozen French-cut
    green beans, thawed
Orange peel, optional

Cook desired amount of white and wild rice according to package directions. In a medium frying pan, stir fry cooked chopped chicken in butter until chicken is heated throughout. In a medium saucepan over medium heat, combine cold water and cornstarch, stirring until cornstarch dissolves. Bring mixture to a boil, stirring frequently, until thickened. Turn off heat and mix in orange marmalade, stirring until evenly blended. Pour orange marmalade mixture over cooked chicken pieces in frying pan. Add salt to taste. When rice has finished cooking, stir in French-cut green beans until mixture is about 1/4 green beans and 3/4 rice. To serve, spread rice and green beans mixture evenly to cover bottom of serving plates. Top with orange glazed chicken pieces. If desired, garnish plates with pieces of orange peel.

Mason House Inn B&B
Bentonsport, Iowa

Crab Bisque

Makes 6 to 8 servings

1 can cream of
  mushroom soup
1 can cream of asparagus
  soup
1 1/2 soup cans milk

1 C. light cream
1 (6 1/2 oz.) can crab meat,
  drained and flaked
1/4 C. cooking sherry
4 T. butter, divided

In a large saucepan, combine cream of mushroom soup and asparagus soup. Stir in milk and light cream. Heat until just boiling. Add crab meat and continue to heat. Stir in cooking sherry just before serving. Pour into individual bowls and float a pat of butter on top of each serving.

Parsonage on the Green B&B
Lee, Massachusetts

90

Cocalico Quick Corn Chowder

Makes 4 servings

4 slices bacon
1 small onion, sliced
2 medium red potatoes, cubed
2 (24 3/4 oz.) cans creamed corn
1 (12 oz.) can evaporated milk
Salt and pepper
1/2 tsp. dried dillweed

Cut bacon into small pieces and place in a 4-quart saucepan. Sauté bacon until almost cooked and add sliced onions, cooking until onions are transparent. Add cubed potatoes and enough water to cover potatoes. Cook until potatoes are tender but not overcooked. Add creamed corn and evaporated milk. Cook over low until heated throughout, stirring occasionally. Add salt, pepper and dried dillweed to taste.

Cocalico Creek B&B
Denver, Pennsylvania

Broccoli Soup

Make 3 quarts

1 1/3 C. chopped celery
and leaves
1 1/2 C. chopped onions
3 cloves garlic, minced
1/3 C. fresh chopped
parsley
8 C. chicken or
vegetable broth

4 C. chopped broccoli
2 1/2 C. diced potatoes
1 tsp. salt
1/8 tsp. pepper
1/4 tsp. dried thyme
1/4 tsp. nutmeg
1/4 tsp. marjoram
1/4 tsp. dried rosemary

In a large soup pot, combine chopped celery and leaves, chopped onions, minced garlic, chopped parsley, chicken broth, chopped broccoli, diced potatoes, salt, pepper, thyme, nutmeg, marjoram and rosemary. Bring mixture to a boil over medium high heat. Reduce heat, cover and let simmer for 30 minutes.

The Christmas House B&B
Ketchikan, Alaska

Desserts

Irish Potatoes (Candy)

8 oz. cream cheese,
   softened
2 lbs. powdered sugar
7 oz. shredded coconut

1 1/2 T. milk
1/2 tsp. vanilla
3 to 4 T. cinnamon

In a medium bowl, combine cream cheese, powdered sugar, shredded coconut, milk and vanilla. Mix well and roll into small balls. Let chill for 1 hour. In a small bowl, place cinnamon. Roll balls in cinnamon and serve or freeze.

Sheep Hill B&B and Antique Shop
East Earl, Pennsylvania

Brownie Pudding

1 C. flour
2 tsp. baking powder
3/4 C. sugar
1/4 C. plus 2 T. cocoa
    powder, divided
1/2 tsp. salt

1/2 C. milk
1 tsp. vanilla
2 T. liquid shortening
3/4 C. walnuts, optional
3/4 C. brown sugar
1 3/4 C. hot water

Preheat oven to 350°. Into a medium bowl, sift flour, baking powder, sugar, 2 tablespoons cocoa powder and salt. Add milk, vanilla and shortening, mixing until smooth. If desired, mix in walnuts. Pour mixture into a greased 8x8" pan. In a small bowl, combine brown sugar and remaining 1/4 cup cocoa powder and sprinkle over batter. Pour hot water over batter in pan but do not stir. Bake for 40 to 45 minutes.

Cocalico Creek B&B
Denver, Pennsylvania

Lemon Cookies

1 lemon cake mix
1 egg
1 (8 oz.) container
   whipped topping

Powdered sugar

Preheat oven to 325°. In a large bowl, combine lemon cake mix, egg and whipped topping. Mix thoroughly until dough is sticky and stiff. Drop dough by teaspoonful into a small bowl of powdered sugar. Completely coat each cookie and place on an ungreased baking sheet. Bake for no more than 8 to 10 minutes, being careful not to brown cookies. The cookies will be soft and crinkled on top when done. Immediately remove cookies from baking sheet and place on brown paper or a wire rack to cool.

Hillside Farm B&B
Mount Joy, Pennsylvania

Thumb Print Cookies

Makes 4 to 5 dozen

1 C. butter, softened	1 C. finely chopped
1 1/2 C. powdered	black walnuts
sugar, divided	Pinch of salt
1 tsp. vanilla	Frosting for filling
1 3/4 C. flour, sifted	

Preheat oven to 350°. In a large bowl, cream together butter, 1/2 cup powdered sugar and vanilla. Add sifted flour, chopped walnuts and salt. Mix well. Form cookie dough into small 1/2" round balls and place on a lightly greased baking sheet. Press down each ball with thumb to make an indentation. Bake for 15 to 20 minutes, being careful not to over bake. Remove cookies from oven and let cool. Shake cooled cookies in remaining 1 cup powdered sugar, being careful not to fill thumbprints. Fill each cookie with 1/2 teaspoon frosting.

Lighthouse Valleyview B&B Inn
Dubuque, Iowa

Chunky Oatmeal Macadamia Cookies

Makes about 5 dozen

1 (18 1/4 oz.) pkg.
  yellow cake mix
1 C. flour
3/4 C. butter, melted
2 eggs
1 tsp. vanilla

1 C. quick oats
1 C. chopped
  macadamia nuts
1 C. white chocolate
  baking chips

Preheat oven to 375°. Grease baking sheets and set aside. In a large mixing bowl, combine yellow cake mix, flour, melted butter, eggs and vanilla. Beat at low speed for 1 minute. Scrape sides of bowl and increase to medium speed for an additional minute. Dough should be thick. Fold in oats, chopped macadamia nuts and white chocolate baking chips. Drop heaping teaspoonfuls of dough, 2" apart, onto prepared baking sheets. Bake for 12 to 14 minutes, until edges are golden brown. Let cookies cool on baking sheets before transferring to wire racks.

The Christmas House B&B
Ketchikan, Alaska

98

Valley Farms' Very Best Chocolate Chip Cookies

Makes 1 1/2 dozen

5 1/2 oz. butter, softened
1 egg
1/2 tsp. vanilla
1/2 tsp. water
1/2 C. sugar
1/2 C. brown sugar

1/4 tsp. salt
1 tsp. baking soda
1 2/3 C. flour, sifted
1/2 C. shredded coconut
1/2 C. chopped pecans
8 oz. chocolate chips

Preheat oven to 375°. In a large mixing bowl, combine butter, egg, vanilla, water, sugar, brown sugar, salt and baking soda. Beat at medium speed until blended. Add sifted flour and mix well. Mix in shredded coconut, chopped pecans and chocolate chips. Bake for 12 minutes, until golden brown.

Inn at Valley Farms B&B and Cottages
Walpole, New Hampshire

99

Matthew's Favorite Peanut Butter Cookies

1/2 C. butter, softened
1/2 C. sugar
3/4 C. brown sugar
3/4 C. peanut butter, any kind

1 egg
1 tsp. vanilla
1 3/4 C. flour
1/2 tsp. baking soda

Preheat oven to 375°. In a large bowl, cream together butter, sugar and brown sugar until mixture is light and fluffy. Blend in peanut butter, egg and vanilla. Add flour and baking soda and mix well. Shape dough into balls and roll in sugar. Place cookies on an ungreased baking sheet and bake for 10 to 12 minutes.

Bear Paw Inn... a B&B
Winter Park, Colorado

100

Nana's Scone Recipe

2 3/4 C. flour	1 egg
1/2 tsp. baking soda	1 C. vanilla yogurt
1/2 tsp. salt	1/2 tsp. vanilla
1/4 C. sugar	1/2 C. raisins or dried fruit
3 tsp. baking powder	2 tsp. milk
1 C. butter, softened	Additional sugar for topping

Preheat oven to 425°. In a large bowl, combine flour, baking soda, salt, sugar and baking powder. Using a pastry blender, cut in butter until mixture is crumbly. Stir in egg, yogurt, vanilla and raisins. Mix just to combine ingredients. Turn dough out onto a floured surface. Knead 6 to 8 times. Form dough into a 9" square. Cut into four small squares and cut each square diagonally into four triangles. Brush scones with milk and sprinkle with sugar. Place scones on a lightly greased baking sheet. Bake for 12 to 15 minutes.

The Dominion House B&B
Blooming Grove, New York

Glazed Lemon Bars

1 1/2 C. plus 2 T.
  Bisquick baking mix,
  divided
3/4 C. plus 3 T. powdered
  sugar, divided
5 T. butter or margarine,
  softened

1 1/2 C. sugar
1 T. grated lemon peel
1/4 C. plus 1 T. plus
  1 1/2 tsp. lemon juice,
  divided
4 eggs

Preheat oven to 350°. In a medium bowl, combine 1 1/2 cups Bisquick and 3 tablespoons powdered sugar. Using a pastry blender, cut in butter until mixture is crumbly. Press mixture into the bottom of an ungreased 9x13" baking dish. Bake 10 minutes, until light brown. In a separate bowl, combine sugar, remaining 2 tablespoons Bisquick, grated lemon peel, 1/4 cup lemon juice and eggs. Pour mixture into baking dish. Bake for 25 minutes, until set and golden brown. While still warm, loosen edges from sides of pan. Meanwhile, in a small bowl, combine remaining 3/4 cup powdered sugar and remaining 1 tablespoon plus 1 1/2 teaspoons lemon juice. Mix until smooth. Spread mixture over baked lemon bars. Let cool completely before cutting into bars.

Sheep Hill B&B and Antique Shop
East Earl, Pennsylvania

O'Henry Bars

4 C. oats
1 C. brown sugar
2/3 C. butter, melted
3 tsp. vanilla

1/2 C. corn syrup
6 oz. chocolate chips
2/3 C. creamy or
    crunchy peanut butter

Preheat oven to 375°. In a large bowl, combine oats, brown sugar, melted butter, vanilla and corn syrup. Spread mixture into a lightly greased 9x13" baking dish. Bake for 12 minutes. Remove from oven and let cool on a wire rack. In a double boiler or medium saucepan over low medium heat, melt together chocolate chips and peanut butter. Mix until smooth and spread over cooled bars.

Canyon Road Inn B&B
Turtle Lake, Wisconsin

Jeanne's Pumpkin Squares

1 box spice cake mix   **1 (16 oz.) can pumpkin**

Preheat oven to 350°. In a large bowl, combine spice cake mix and pumpkin. With a hand mixer, beat mixture until completely combined. Spread batter into a greased 9x12" baking dish. Bake for 30 minutes or until a toothpick inserted in the center of cake comes out clean.

Blue Ball B&B
Blue Ball, Pennsylvania

Banana Cream Pie

2/3 C. sugar
1/4 C. cornstarch
1/2 tsp. salt
3 C. milk
4 egg yolks, slightly
    beaten

2 T. butter, softened
1 T. plus 1 tsp. vanilla
2 large bananas, peeled
    and sliced
1 (9") baked pie crust
3 to 5 C. whipped cream

In a large saucepan, combine sugar, cornstarch and salt. In a medium bowl, combine milk and egg yolks and gradually stir into sugar mixture. Cook over medium heat, stirring constantly, until mixture thickens and boils. Boil and stir for an additional minute. Remove from heat and add butter and vanilla. Mix well. Cover mixture with plastic wrap and let cool to room temperature. Place sliced bananas in 9" baked pie crust. Pour room temperature filling over bananas. Top with whipped cream.

Cocalico Creek B&B
Denver, Pennsylvania

Coconut Pineapple Pie

Makes 6 servings

1 C. sugar	3 eggs, beaten
3 T. flour	1 tsp. vanilla
1 C. light corn syrup	1 frozen pie crust
1 C. shredded coconut	1/4 C. butter or
1 (8 oz.) can crushed	margarine, melted
pineapple in juice	

Preheat oven to 350°. In a medium bowl, combine sugar and flour. Add corn syrup, shredded coconut, crushed pineapple in juice, beaten eggs and vanilla. Mix until well blended. Pour mixture into frozen pie crust. Drizzle melted butter over pie. Bake for 50 to 55 minutes, until a knife inserted in the center comes out clean. If desired, cover edge of pie crust loosely with aluminum foil to prevent from browning. Let cool on a wire rack. Chill in refrigerator before cutting into slices. Store pie in refrigerator.

Rock Cottage Gardens... a Bed & Breakfast Inn
Eureka Springs, Arkansas

Mocha Pecan Pie

1 C. chocolate chips
3 T. Kahlua liqueur
3 large eggs, beaten
1/2 C. brown sugar
1 C. light corn syrup
2 tsp. vanilla

1/4 tsp. salt
1/2 C. butter, melted
1 1/4 C. coarsely chopped
    pecans, toasted*, divided
1 (9") unbaked pie crust

Preheat oven to 350°. In a double boiler, combine chocolate chips and Kahlua. Heat until chocolate is melted and set aside. In a large mixing bowl, combine beaten eggs, brown sugar, corn syrup, vanilla and salt. Beat at medium speed for 1 minute, until blended. Stir in melted chocolate mixture. Mix in melted butter and 1 cup toasted pecans, mixing until evenly blended. Pour mixture into pie crust. Sprinkle remaining 1/4 cup toasted pecans over top of pie. Bake for 45 minutes, until center of pie is almost set. Pie will continue to set as it cools.

* To toast, place chopped pecans in a single layer on a baking sheet. Bake at 350° for approximately 10 minutes or until pecans are golden brown.

The White Rose B&B Inn
Wisconsin Dells, Wisconsin

Peach Cobbler

Makes 8 servings

1 1/2 C. flour	3/4 C. milk
1 1/2 C. sugar	1 tsp. vanilla
1 1/2 tsp. baking powder	8 C. canned or fresh
1 tsp. salt	peaches, drained
1 tsp. cinnamon	8 oz. heavy whipping cream
8 T. butter, softened, cut	8 oz. peach yogurt
into pieces	

Preheat oven to 350°. In a blender or food processor, place flour, sugar, baking powder, salt and cinnamon. Pulse until well blended. Using a pastry blender, cut in butter until mixture is crumbly. Transfer mixture to a large bowl and add milk and vanilla. Mix well. Grease the bottom and sides of 8 (1 cup) ramekins or a 9x13" glass baking dish. Dust each ramekin or baking dish with cinnamon and sugar. Spoon 1 cup peaches into each ramekin or spread peaches evenly over bottom of baking dish. Place 1/4 cup of batter mixture over peaches in each ramekin or spread batter evenly over peaches in baking dish. Bake for 45 minutes. In a medium bowl, beat together heavy whipping cream and peach yogurt until stiff. Before serving, top each ramekin with a spoonful of yogurt mixture or serve on the side with slices from baking dish.

Autumn Pond B&B
Leavenworth, Washington

Cherry Crumb Crunch

1/2 C. butter or
    margarine, melted
3/4 C. brown sugar
3/4 tsp. salt
3/4 C. quick oats

1 1/2 C. flour
1/2 tsp. baking powder
3/4 C. chopped walnuts
1 can cherry filling

Preheat oven to 350°. In a large bowl, combine melted butter, brown sugar, salt, oats, flour, baking powder and chopped walnuts. Place half of the mixture in a greased 9x13" glass baking dish and firmly press down. Spread cherry filling evenly over crust. Sprinkle remaining half of crumb mixture over cherry filling. Bake for 30 minutes.

Variation
Can substitute 2 cups fresh cherries thickened with 1/2 to 3/4 cup sugar, 3 tablespoons flour and 1/4 teaspoon cinnamon for the can of cherry filling.

Walnut Lawn B&B
Lancaster, Pennsylvania

Peach Berry Crisp

Makes 8 servings

4 C. peeled and cut fresh peaches	1/2 C. flour
1 C. berries, such as blueberries, raspberries or mixed	1/2 C. quick oats
	1 tsp. cinnamon
	1/2 tsp. nutmeg
3/4 C. brown sugar	1/3 C. butter or oleo, softened
	1/2 C. chopped pecans

Preheat oven to 375°. Grease an 8x8" baking dish and arrange cut peaches and berries evenly over bottom of pan. In a large bowl, combine brown sugar, flour, oats, cinnamon, nutmeg, butter and chopped pecans. Mix well and sprinkle mixture evenly over fruit in pan. Bake for 30 to 40 minutes, until topping is lightly browned. If desired, serve warm with ice cream or whipped topping.

Tunnel Mountain B&B
Elkins, West Virginia

110

Prime Time Fruit Crisp

1/3 C. sugar
3/4 C. flour, divided
4 to 6 C. fresh fruit,
 any kind

1/2 C. brown sugar
1/2 C. oats
1/2 C. walnuts or pecans
1/2 C. almonds

Preheat oven to 350°. In a large bowl, combine sugar and 1/4 cup flour. Add fruit and toss together. Set aside. In a separate bowl, combine remaining 1/2 cup flour, brown sugar, oats and nuts. Mix thoroughly. Generously grease a baking dish. Spread fruit mixture evenly over bottom of dish. Sprinkle oats and nuts mixture over fruit in pan. Bake for about 45 minutes. Some good fruit combinations are apples and craisins (add 1/2 teaspoon cinnamon to the sugar/flour mixture), peaches and 1/2 pint raspberries, strawberries and rhubarb, or frozen raspberries and canned pears.

Homespun Farm B&B
Griswold, Connecticut

Chocolate Apricot Torte

Makes 12 servings

1 lb. dried and coarsely chopped apricots	1/2 C. chocolate chips
1/2 C. sugar	1/2 tsp. salt
1 1/2 C. water	1 tsp. vanilla
2 T. fresh lemon juice	3/4 C. brown sugar
1 3/4 C. plus 2 T. flour, divided	3/4 C. cold butter, cut into pieces
2 C. walnuts	Chocolate curls, optional

Preheat oven to 350°. To make filling, in a medium saucepan over low heat, combine apricots, sugar, water, lemon juice, and 2 tablespoons flour. Cook about 10 minutes, stirring frequently, until thickened and most of the liquid is absorbed. Remove from heat and let cool. To make dough, in a blender or food processor combine walnuts and chocolate chips and pulse until mixture is coarsely chopped. In a large mixing bowl, beat together walnut mixture, remaining 1 3/4 cups flour, salt, vanilla and brown sugar. Using a pastry blender, cut in butter until mixture is crumbly. Place 2/3 of the dough in the bottom and 1 1/2" up sides of a 9 1/2" springform pan. Spread filling evenly over crust and crumble remaining 1/3 dough over filling. Bake for 50 to 60 minutes, until golden brown. Remove to a wire rack and let torte cool completely in pan before removing sides of springform pan. If desired, garnish top of torte with chocolate curls. Torte may be made up to 1 day ahead, covered and chilled in refrigerator until ready to serve.

Rock Cottage Gardens… a Bed & Breakfast Inn
Eureka Springs, Arkansas

Swedish Pastry

2 C. flour, sifted, divided
1 C. butter, softened, divided
1 C. plus 2 T. water, divided

1/4 C. sugar
3 eggs
2 tsp. almond extract, divided
1/2 to 1 C. powdered sugar

Preheat oven to 350°. In a medium bowl, combine 1 cup sifted flour, 1/2 cup butter and 2 tablespoons water with a pastry blender. Mix until dough resembles pie crust and spread dough into a shallow greased 9x13" baking dish or jellyroll pan. In a medium saucepan over medium heat, combine remaining 1 cup water, sugar and remaining 1/2 cup butter. Bring to a boil and remove from heat. Quickly stir in remaining 1 cup sifted flour, making sure lumps do not form. Add eggs, one at a time, beating well after each addition. Stir in 1 teaspoon almond extract and mix until well blended. Spread mixture over crust in prepared pan. Bake for 55 to 60 minutes. In a medium bowl, combine powdered sugar and remaining 1 teaspoon almond extract. Frost cooled pastry with powdered sugar mixture. If desired, decorate pastry with sliced almonds, chopped maraschino cherries or colored sugar.

Canyon Road Inn B&B
Turtle Lake, Wisconsin

Apple Strudel Waterloo

2 lbs. apples, peeled, cored and chopped	2 T. rum
1/2 C. sugar	1/2 C. pine nuts or hazelnuts
1 tsp. cinnamon	1 sheet puff pastry
2/3 C. raisins	1 to 2 egg yolks, beaten

Preheat oven to 375°. In a large saucepan over low heat, steep apples, sugar, cinnamon, raisins, rum and nuts until softened. Roll out puff pastry on a flat, lightly floured cloth. Stretch out pastry with hands until paper thin. Trim edges of pastry if they are thick or uneven. Distribute apple mixture evenly over pastry. Lift side of cloth little by little until puff pastry rolls up and over filling. Transfer strudel to a lightly greased baking sheet and press edges of pastry together along sides. Coat pastry with beaten egg yolks. Bake for 30 minutes, until browned and crisp. To serve, cut strudel into slices and serve with vanilla sauce or over vanilla ice cream.

Waterloo Country Inn
Princess Anne, Maryland

The Very Best Sour Cream Coffee Cake

3 C. flour
1 1/2 tsp. baking powder
1 1/2 tsp. baking soda
1/4 tsp. salt
1 1/2 C. butter, softened
1 1/2 C. sugar
4 eggs
1 1/2 C. sour cream

2 T. plus 1 1/2 tsp. vanilla,
   divided
3/4 C. brown sugar
1 1/2 tsp. cinnamon
1 1/2 tsp. nutmeg
1 C. finely chopped walnut
   or pecans
2 T. water

Preheat oven to 325°. Grease a 10" tube pan. In a medium bowl, sift together flour, baking powder, baking soda and salt. Set aside. In a separate bowl, beat together butter and sugar until fluffy. Add eggs, beating carefully after each one. Add sour cream and 1 1/2 teaspoons vanilla. Gradually add dry ingredients and beat well. In a separate bowl, combine brown sugar, cinnamon, nutmeg and nuts. Pour 1/3 of the batter into prepared pan. Sprinkle with half of the nut mixture. Add another 1/3 of the batter and cover with remaining nut mix. Add remaining batter, spreading so edges are sealed to the pan. In a small bowl, mix remaining 2 tablespoons vanilla with water. Pour mixture over top of batter. Bake for 70 minutes. Let cool for 10 minutes before removing from pan. The coffee cake should remain moist for days.

The Pillars B&B
Plainfield, New Jersey

Knobby Apple Cake

1 C. flour
1/2 tsp. baking powder
1/2 tsp. baking soda
1/2 tsp. salt
1/2 tsp. cinnamon
1/2 tsp. nutmeg
1/4 C. shortening

1 C. sugar
1 egg, beaten
3 C. apples, cut into
   1/2" cubes
1/4 C. chopped nuts,
   optional
1 tsp. vanilla

Preheat oven to 350°. Into a medium bowl, sift flour, baking powder, baking soda, salt, cinnamon and nutmeg. In a separate bowl, cream together shortening and sugar. Add beaten egg. Add diced apples, chopped nuts, vanilla and sifted dry ingredients. Mix well. Batter will seem dry at first, but will take moisture from the apples. Transfer batter to a greased 8" square pan. Bake for 45 minutes. Serve warm or cold. If desired, serve with whipped cream or ice cream. Cake freezes well.

Harmony Hill B&B
Arrington, Virginia

Rhubarb Cake

1 C. margarine, softened
3 C. brown sugar
2 eggs
2 C. buttermilk
2 tsp. baking soda
1 tsp. salt

1 tsp. vanilla
4 C. flour
4 C. chopped rhubarb
1 C. sugar
2 tsp. cinnamon

Preheat oven to 350°. In a large bowl, combine margarine, brown sugar, eggs and buttermilk. Mix in baking soda, salt, vanilla, flour and chopped rhubarb. Stir until evenly blended. Pour mixture into a greased 11x15" baking dish. To make topping, in a small bowl, combine sugar and cinnamon. Sprinkle mixture over batter in pan. Bake for 40 minutes. Serve warm or cold with butter, vanilla ice cream, whipped cream or warm rum raisin sauce.

Mason House Inn B&B
Bentonsport, Iowa

Carrot Cake Waterloo

5 eggs, separated
1 T. grated lemon peel
1 1/2 C. sugar
1 1/3 C. shredded carrots
1 1/3 C. ground almonds
4 T. flour or cornstarch
1/2 tsp. cinnamon
Pinch of ground cloves

1 tsp. baking powder
Pinch of salt
2 T. Kirsch schnapps or rum
3 T. apricot marmalade
1 1/2 C. powdered sugar
1/2 egg white
2 T. lemon juice or
    schnapps

Preheat oven to 375°. In a medium bowl, combine egg yolks, grated lemon peel and sugar until creamy. Fold in shredded carrots and almonds. Add flour, cinnamon, ground cloves, baking powder and salt. Beat 5 egg whites to soft peaks. Pour schnapps or rum into dough and fold in egg whites. Pour dough into a lightly greased 9" springform pan. Bake for 60 minutes. Spread apricot marmalade over warm cake. Once cooled, remove sides of pan. In a medium bowl, combine powdered sugar, 1/2 egg white and lemon juice. Pour glaze over marmalade and spread in a circular motion over tops and sides of cake.

Waterloo Country Inn
Princess Anne, Maryland

Bed & Breakfast Contributors

The Christmas House B&B
Ketchikan, Alaska
907-247-2489

La Paz in Desert Springs B&B
Scottsdale, Arizona
888-922-0963

Empress of Little Rock B&B
Little Rock, Arkansas
501-374-7966

Rock Cottage Gardens...
    a Bed & Breakfast Inn
Eureka Springs, Arkansas
800-624-6646

Packard House B&B
Mendocino, California
888-453-2677

Bear Paw Inn...a B&B
Winter Park, Colorado
970-887-1351

Deacon Timothy Pratt B&B
Old Saybrook, Connecticut
800-640-1195

Homespun Farm B&B
Griswold, Connecticut
888-889-6673

River House B&B Inn & Tepee
Rockford-Machesney Park, Illinois
815-636-1884

Sassafras Ridge B&B
Carbondale, Illinois
618-529-5261

The Steamboat House B&B
Galena, Illinois
815-777-2317

Calmar Guesthouse B&B
Calmar, Iowa
563-562-3851

Lighthouse Valleyview B&B Inn
Dubuque, Iowa
800-407-7023

Mason House Inn B&B
Bentonsport, Iowa
800-592-3133

Aleksander House B&B
Louisville, Kentucky
502-637-4985

Maison Louisiane Historic B&B
Natchitoches, Louisiana
800-264-8991

Waterloo Country Inn
Princess Anne, Maryland
410-651-0883

B&B Associates Bay Colony
Boston, Massachusetts
800-347-5088

Parsonage on the Green B&B
Lee, Massachusetts
413-243-4364

Martha's Vineyard B&B
South Haven, Michigan
269-637-9373

Magnolia Grove B&B
Hernando, Mississippi
866-404-2626

Atwood House B&B
Lincoln, Nebraska
800-884-6554

Highland Lake Inn, B&B
East Andover, New Hampshire
603-735-6426

Inn at Valley Farms B&B and
    Cottages
Walpole, New Hampshire
603-756-2855

119

The Pillars B&B
Plainfield, New Jersey
908-753-0922

Big Moose Inn B&B
Eagle Bay, New York
315-357-2042

The Dominion House B&B
Blooming Grove, New York
845-496-1826

Good Life Inn B&B
High Rolls, New Mexico
866-LIFE-INN

Elson Inn B&B
Magnolia, Ohio
330-866-9242

Cliff House B&B
Waldport, Oregon
541-563-2506

Amanda Gish House B&B
Elizabethtown, Pennsylvania
866-401-0889

Blue Ball B&B
Blue Ball, Pennsylvania
717-355-9994

Cocalico Creek B&B
Denver, Pennsylvania
888-208-7334

Hillside Farm B&B
Mount Joy, Pennsylvania
717-653-6697

Sheep Hill B&B and Antique Shop
East Earl, Pennsylvania
800-557-7750

Walnut Lawn B&B
Lancaster, Pennsylvania
717-464-1382

Sunrise Farm B&B
Salem, South Carolina
888-991-0121

Iron Mountain Inn B&B and
    Creekside Chalet
Butler, Tennessee
888-781-2399

Roses & the River Inc. B&B
Brazoria, Texas
800-610-1070

Frog Hollow B&B
Lexington, Virginia
540-463-5444

Harmony Hill B&B
Arrington, Virginia
877-263-7750

Autumn Pond B&B
Leavenworth, Washington
800-222-9661

Chambered Nautilus B&B Inn
Seattle, Washington
800-545-8459

Dupont at The Circle - a B&B Inn
Washington, D.C.
202-332-5251

Tunnel Mountain B&B and
    Riverside Retreat
Elkins, West Virginia
304-636-1684

Canyon Road Inn B&B
Turtle Lake, Wisconsin
888-251-5542

The White Rose B&B Inn
Wisconsin Dells, Wisconsin
800-482-4724

Nagle Warren Mansion B&B
Cheyenne, Wyoming
800-811-2610

Index

Beverages, Sauces & Snacks

Breads & Sides

Main Dishes & Soups

Desserts